P9-DGI-400

PERFECT CITY

An Urban Fixer's Global Search for Magic in the Modern Metropolis

JOE BERRIDGE

sh.
SUTHERLAND
HOUSE

Sutherland House
416 Moore Ave., Suite 205
Toronto, ON M4G 109

First hardcover edition, May 2019

If you are interested in inviting one of our authors to a live event or media appearance, please contact publicity@sutherlandhousebooks.com and visit our website at sutherlandhousebooks.com for more information about our authors and their schedules.

Manufactured in Canada
Cover designed by Shubhani Sarkar
Cover photograph courtesy Shutterstock
Book composed by Karl Hunt

Library and Archives Canada Cataloguing in Publication
Title: Perfect city / by Joe Berridge.
Names: Berridge, Joe, 1946- author.
Description: Includes index.
Identifiers: Canadiana 20190043784 |
ISBN 9781999439514 (hardcover)
Subjects: LCSH: Berridge, Joe, 1946—Travel. |
LCSH: City planners—Travel. | LCSH: City planning. |
LCSH: Cities and towns.
Classification: LCC HT166 B47 2019 |
DDC 307.1/216—dc23

ISBN 978-1-9994395-1-4

To Billie

CONTENTS

1

PERFECT CITY

Perfect city? That's absurd. There is no such thing, any more than there are perfect people. But cities, like people, do have perfect moments. They attain perfection here and there in different ways and it is these moments of perfection we hope to experience when we visit the great cities of the world. It is these moments we strive to create in the building of our own cities. And it is these moments that we have in mind when we search for the perfect place to work and raise a family, the perfect skyscraper or urban beach, the perfect city park or open-air market, the perfect place to sit with a coffee and enjoy the unique life of the city around us.

In recent times, the search for urban perfection has become more complex, more serious. The world is urbanizing at a dizzying rate, the biggest cities fastest of all. They now rival nation states as the places where the social, economic, environmental and political future of the planet will be resolved. The list of issues facing civic leaders is endless. What constitutes the best urban transit system, the best high school? How can we most productively settle new immigrants in the city, or deal most practically with the implications of climate change? What is the best strategy to stimulate urban innovation, to green the city, to bring back broken neighborhoods, to mitigate income inequality, to get people out of their cars, to run a city government that actually gets things done? Figure all this out and you would have the perfect city, but no one municipality is close to delivering it all.

It used to be easier. Much of what we like or admire in the great cities was produced by kings or potentates or all-powerful city bosses: The Prince Regent, Baron Haussmann, Robert Moses, Lee Kuan Yew. In the second half of the last century that top-down vision of urban perfection came to a crashing halt when the writer and activist Jane Jacobs stood in front of bulldozers in New York and brought the expressway construction promoted by her nemesis Robert Moses, the master city builder of mid-century New York, to a standstill. She repeated that same victory just a few years later in Toronto. A new vision of the perfect city was born, one that emphasized bottom-up, community-led, organically driven economic development. Jacob's vision remains to this day the predominant way of thinking about how to make good cities. Yet it too has its shortcomings. Effective, perhaps, at the local level, but it lacks the confidence and competence to tackle the big challenges of the modern megalopolis. There is no organic way to build a massive, integrated, efficient and affordable transportation system, or to plan a new airport, or to develop a new financial district. Suspicion of big ideas about cities, and erosion of the concentration of power necessary to make them happen, has led to lost decades of urban investment in many European and North American cities. All of this leaves us at a critical time in the practice of city building without a single dominant model for undertaking the task. That is not all bad. Rather, we are seeing fresh energy and experimentation in cities around the world, and an unprecedented global exchange of ideas, strategies and projects. The perfect city is being born the world over. It is this fascinating urban ferment and the resultant, exhilarating new searches for urban perfection that inspired this book.

* * *

Any conversation about perfectibility needs to begin with an understanding of the essential nature of the entity under consideration—the city. I work in and on cities all over the world and stand in awe of their vast complexity, their remarkable differences and yet their intriguing similarities. As a city planner, I think of myself as a kind of urban mechanic. Each city is a machine I am trying to fix, and each needs to be approached with a measure of humility because each has a life of its own. While cities are first of all machines, physical objects, they share a metabolism with their human inhabitants and the natural world. They are machines driven by the dynamics of history, geography, technology, environmental change and the global economy. Like every other living thing, they have patterns of growth and decline, regeneration and death, partly subject to human tinkering but in an equally important sense almost independent of our interventions, with dynamics all their own. Often times, modern cities seem almost to be making themselves, with those in charge, the perfection seekers, struggling for a mere semblance of control over what is happening. They cannot be planned so much as they can be nudged, patched, or pushed, especially today as the ever-accelerating pace of urban change shifts into overdrive. An urban mechanic can only be effective by acknowledging the power of these forces. You cannot confront them; you have to work with them as best you can.

Like any other machine, a great city is purpose built. The first task of the urban machine is to create and distribute wealth. It is on the economic prosperity of a city that all its other attributes depend. Living in Toronto, one of the most economically successful cities in the modern world, it is easy to forget how fundamental the creation of wealth is to the metropolis, along with the key processes of distributing that wealth through new jobs, investment in transit and service infrastructure, and the provision of community benefits like parks, schools and libraries. Wealth engenders a sense of hope and possibility in people. For the increasingly immigrant city, as most global metropolises now are, the prospect of a good job is the key bargain between the city and its new citizen. Without that, nothing but trouble lies ahead. A city's ability to generate wealth improves and declines partly in response to wider economic forces but also due to the quality of its management. *Perfect City* will take you to cities that have struggled, and are still struggling, with their ability to create new wealth for their residents. It will share those cities' strategies for urban prosperity and their perplexity with that particular quandary of the modern urban economy, its tendency, the more economically successful it becomes, to exacerbate a greater divide between rich and poor.

Cities are also machines for moving things around. People. Food. Water. Sewage. Electricity. Garbage. Goods. Bikes. Cars. Ideas. The amount of movement seems to increase exponentially as a city gets larger. These moving parts—the roads, transit systems, tunnels and bridges, sewers and water pipes, heating and cooling systems, fiber-optic cable—are all aging and decaying at the same time as new demands are being put on them. And the technology and business model that underpins them is itself in flux. The taxi system collapses in the face of Uber and Lyft, the urban energy demand shifts towards renewable sources. Some cities are introducing road tolls, others bike lanes, and still others both. All cities are trying to update their transit systems in the face of rapidly changing trends; some can and some can't. The urban machine evolves sometimes gradually and sometimes with a jolt, even as those tunnels and bridges, roads and tracks inexorably decay. The urban mechanic scarcely knows which way to turn.

Uniquely, the urban machine also provides a home, the place where we humans now predominantly live. The creation of home, in the full sense of that word, is another basic task of any city. The search for home is one of the most powerful drivers in our lives and the perfect city must provide that essential sense of security and welcome, that benign domesticity for which we all search. It needs to accommodate us night and day as we raise our children, look after our parents, care for our neighborhoods, walk around after sundown, and soundly sleep. It must connect us with jobs and life partners, and comfort us in our life struggles, whether we seek to make a fortune or simply to pay the rent. It needs to provide us with all the amenities of modern life, the urban equivalent of household appliances: parks, schools, libraries, office and retail spaces, hospitals and educational institutions. And it must do this for a stunning diversity of people. One of the most formidable challenges in city building today is how to make the city a home in which both long-term residents and a flood of newcomers from all over the planet can reside as productively, harmoniously and joyously as possible. The tides of urban in-migration have never been stronger, creating a historically unique human environment in the modern metropolis. The world's big cities now typically have about a third of their population made up by new migrants from other countries, some as much as a half. Urban diversity at such a scale has never happened before and these population flows are not going to diminish. The perfect city has to release the energy of this new human capital and at the same time turn its immigrants into citizens. The top dozen global cities also have to contend with severe stresses in their housing markets, with prices that threaten to choke that key supply of labor on which they depend. Many of the cities we will be visiting are struggling with how to build fast enough to keep up with demand and still provide for those on lower incomes.

Finally, a great city is a place of enduring delight. People move to cities not just for functional reasons and material opportunity but because cities are and always have been the greatest of human creations. Urban delight is not a conventional aesthetic. It goes far deeper than a painting or a performance. It involves the look, the sound, the smell of the city, the movement of its streets, the dynamic interactions of person and place, of solids and voids. It does not follow the normal rules. Some cities enchant you with their regenerated waterfronts, or with memorable or provocative architecture. But just as often delight is found in the strangest of places, in the corners of the city, in its leftover and hidden backs and fronts. Urban delight, as we shall see, can even be ugly. It comes in myriad forms—which is just as well, since over half the world's population now lives and works in big cities and calls such places home. We might as well all find something to enjoy.

* * *

Perfect City starts where I started as a city planner and still live and happily call home, a place not that well known to the rest of the world, one that has arrived somewhat accidentally to the role of megalopolis, the perfectly imperfect city of Toronto. We move on to

New York—where else but to the current capital city of the world, the focus of today's economic and cultural power, to study how that most impressive of mayors, Michael Bloomberg, reframed its future. We will visit London, a city that regained its upward trajectory after decades of post-war decline, boldly rebuilding and extending its transit lines, staging a successful Olympics and managing a dramatic improvement in educational outcomes for its increasingly diverse population, but now facing a gravely uncertain future following the Brexit vote.

Any thinking about the global urban future has to get away from the west and observe, with awe and uncertainty, cities such as Singapore, which has vaulted to the top of the global urban hierarchy in its own distinctive way—an approach that has forced me to reconsider mine— and to exploding Shanghai, soon to be larger than New York, London and Singapore put together, a city whose scale, energy and effectiveness should make it capital of the world by the end of the century.

The crucial function for any big city has always been to accommodate newcomers from other countries or from the countryside, turning them into contented, productive citizens. Toronto and Sydney, two of the most culturally diverse, economically vibrant and remarkably harmonious cities in the world are distant cousins in the creation of a practical urban social democracy. Both are in the process of inventing a new, post-ethnic culture of urban citizenship, a distinctive new version of home.

And then there are cities struggling with unique challenges: Belfast, trying to find civic harmony after the worst thing that can happen to a city, an urban civil war; and Manchester, energetically re-inventing its economic machine, culture and football teams after industrial collapse and a devastating act of terrorism that obliterated much of its urban core. We will see how each of these smaller cities is working to remain relevant in a world in which fewer and fewer global cities seem more and more dominant.

I have been fortunate to spend my working life as an urban insider. As an international urban consultant, I have competed in the high-energy, high-risk global market for ideas on cities and their futures. I have sat with city mayors and managers, architects and activists, developers and entrepreneurs, citizens and community groups, as they searched for urban perfection. One of the most remarkable conclusions as a city builder is that despite—or perhaps because of—the complexity of great cities, nothing of substance happens unless one individual makes it happen. I will introduce you to some of these remarkable people, and the policies and programs, strategies and solutions that different big cities are employing to remain competitive, equitable and sustainable.

Above all else, I want to share my love for cities with readers as we walk through their backs and fronts, their centers and suburbs, as we sample their stores and restaurants, upscale and down market, their public facilities, their cultural offerings, their recreations and, of course, their street theater. You must see the center of any city, but you must also get out of the center and travel to the end of the subway line, to the outskirts where many of my most fascinating projects have been, to the home of the urban precariat, to the low end of income inequality, where in many ways the future of the perfect city will be resolved for good or ill. We will contrast and compare the wealthiest and the poorest neighborhoods of New York, London and Toronto, and we will spend perhaps an inordinate amount of time in public libraries, one of the least appreciated yet most important elements of urban infrastructure.

No discussion of urban life can avoid the subject of city government. Municipalities are traditionally the junior level of government, beneath national and state or provincial legislatures. City hall has traditionally been disdained as parochial, petty, and corrupt. Local councils are often figures of fun. Yet some smart municipal governments and their host countries are realizing that if cities truly are the engines of the new economy, the critical entry point for immigration and the place where national cultures and values are increasingly set, then how cities are managed is of central importance to the welfare of the whole. City government has to be simultaneously big and small—big enough to manage large transportation systems, housing affordability, public safety and major economic development projects, and yet small enough to engage directly with its citizens to whose homes it delivers so many local services. Many of the cities I have worked in are struggling to find the right balance between necessary structural initiatives and smaller, more intimate interventions, and some are failing because they cannot.

As a city planner, I have worked in and on many of the world's great cities, and some of the not so great, as they strive for perfection. *Perfect City* is also about my life in those cities and about what I have seen and learned along the way. I am an urban practitioner, not a theorist, suspicious of those with elaborate theories on urban planning. Cities are as complicated as life itself. Planners operate in the space between city government, private investment and individual citizens, a tricky game of middle ground and compromise. Unlike theoreticians, or look-at-me architects, planners are joined in a profession of modesty. How can you really direct the future of cities that are the product of such powerful forces, that are the repositories of so many domestic dreams, and whose delights are often more a consequence of accident than intention? My profession falls way short of a science but, done effectively, it can be an art. I will share my joys, confusions, struggles, successes and failures in pursuit of that art.

Fortunately for me, many smart people have themselves wrestled with these questions about the perfectibility of urban life. We will meet important writers, city builders and researchers as we conduct our global tour. Front of the line has to be the pair that still struggles for the soul of the city: the writer and activist Jane Jacobs and her nemesis, Robert Moses, the master builder of post-war New York. Jacobs, a long-time friend and neighbor in Toronto, taught us that the organic power of a city is its key source of wealth and happiness. Moses taught us what it takes to harness money and power to instigate large-scale urban change, to actually get things done that make a difference. The conflict between them and their ideas has endured half a century, and at some points it has tended towards caricature, but it remains instructive and it is the starting point for our discussion of where cities are headed in the future. We will meet my colleague at the University of Toronto, Richard Florida, perhaps today's most astute observer of the drivers of the modern city, and Dr. Cheong Koon Hean, the Singaporean civil servant who put her finger on the key ingredient for her city's remarkable success: "All we have is brains."

A final note. I like to eat, good food being the most reliable measure of urban health, and my greatest source of urban delight. So our analysis of our urban future and our tours of exemplary cities will usually culminate in a visit to a favorite restaurant, whether an Asian street market, a New York oyster bar or an Irish pub, where we can continue our conversation.

2

PATRON SAINT
OF THE CITY

I was brought up in an English county town, an Agatha Christie kind of place, the kind for which Miss Marple would put on a hat when calling upon her solicitor. The famed crime writer actually lived just a few villages away, a busy, sensible woman who served on the local school board. But then I read about cities, about places that could not have been more different. Jane Jacobs' *Death and Life of Great American Cities* was almost the first book, and certainly the most influential, that I read at university in England. I was struck, not just by its obvious good sense but by its passions, its engagement, its description of the active, dark power of a city.

I was of the age and *Death and Life* was the book of the times, an unanswerable critique of an earlier generation's city planners. How clear their errors, how misguided their intentions, how craven their misdeeds. How much more authentic the improvised drama of the street than their bureaucratic interventions. The book was a call to arms, right up there on the shelf with such game-changing manifestos as Rachel Carson's *Silent Spring*, which initiated the contemporary environmental movement, and Betty Friedan's *The Feminine Mystique*, which pointed to new ways for women to live in the world. All three written by utterly original American women, all published in a spurt in the early 1960s, and all a part of our generation's narrative with an influence that carries to this day.

I knew I had to get to North America where the real cities were. So after the lottery of grad school applications, I ended up in Toronto. I had no idea, when I left the thatched villages of South Devon, that Jane Jacobs had also just moved to Toronto from New York.

I hated the city. Actually, that is too strong because there was really nothing much to hate. Toronto was simply ugly, provincial, ignorant; too cold when it was not, briefly, too hot. I was a European student who had just come through the epochal events of 1968. I had inhaled R.D. Laing and Herbert Marcuse, Frantz Fanon and Germaine Greer, Daniel Cohn-Bendit and Tariq Ali. I was mesmerized by the turmoil in the United States, its Vietnam War, its summer of love, the Martin Luther King and Bobby Kennedy assassinations, by Warhol, Sontag and Mailer. It seemed that no one in Toronto had heard much of this or affected any interest in it. The city was nice and dull. If you wanted a bottle of wine, you wrote a number on a form—1146B, I remember it still—and handed it to the sullen man behind the window who then passed you a bottle of cheap Bulgarian plonk.

My wife and I left Toronto at the earliest opportunity to travel in Central America. We ran out of money and spirit and ended up in New York, living with my mother-in-law in her tiny rent-controlled apartment on the Upper West Side. I phoned a friendly professor at the University of Toronto, the only person I knew who could help us raise the funds to get back to England. He gave me a teaching assistant's job—you could do that then—and we shamefacedly returned to Canada. But in our absence something seemed to have changed or, rather, the scales had fallen from my eyes. Toronto was suddenly in a ferment of urban excitement. At City Hall, David Crombie, soon to be elected mayor, and a group of councilors including another future mayor, John Sewell, were bent on remaking the city. The Union of American Exiles, thousands deep, demonstrated in front of the U.S. Consulate. Joni Mitchell was performing at the Riverboat Coffee House, where Gordon Lightfoot had launched his career. Neil Young was in town as a solo artist. A vibrant Canadian literary movement, centered around the writers Margaret Atwood and Gwendolyn MacEwen, was emerging from the bohemian neighborhood of Yorkville.

Jane Jacobs had arrived in Toronto a year before me because her husband Bob, an architect, had landed a job in the city, and because her two sons could thus avoid the Vietnam draft. Then, incredibly, she suddenly materialized in my U of T seminar room. At the invitation of a longtime activist professor, Jim Lemon, she hijacked my first teaching class, thrust placards into my students' hands and marched us all across campus to the Ontario Legislature at Queen's Park to protest against the Spadina Expressway. Metro Toronto Council had just presented her with the opportunity for an exact reprise of the battle she had won against New York's Crosstown Expressway shortly before leaving the U.S. In relatively short order, the equivalently destructive Spadina Expressway was halted in its ditch. Jane had done it. Toronto was happening.

It was not that I fell in love with the city. I remember, very distinctly, falling in love with a street. Spadina Avenue, the one the expressway would have wrecked. A block even, between Dundas and College, Grossman's and the El Mocambo. It was a couple of years after coming back, a sweet, early summer day, late morning. I was on the east side walking north when I was hit by what the French call *un coup de foudre*. This was the one. And I am still here, urban monogamous. I still love Spadina, every day, a fine-boned mess of a street that remains essentially the same every time it changes completely.

There was not a single one of the Chinese or Vietnamese stores or restaurants that dominate the street today. It was still primarily Jewish, with a strong presence of Hungarian and other Eastern European shops. At the south end, the fur and schmatte businesses were still in full swing. Cars angle-parked, backing out into traffic. Horns, screeches, yells. Then the restaurant explosion arrived out of Chinatown on Dundas Street and the street was transformed. The "fashion district" sank under free trade, its buildings filling with squatters, designers and techies. New separated streetcar tracks arrived, although they were still not quite able to calm the chaos of the street. It was, like all great streets, an ever-changing urban theater with an evolving cast.

What did Jacobs describe as the essence of the perfect city? Ensure a mix of uses, pump up the density, keep blocks short, blend the new with the old, foster local business, promote life on the street, forget about the car, leave good things alone. It was a simple and enduring catechism for urban passion. *Death and Life* became, perhaps still is, the closest thing there is to a bible of modern urban planning. Though it was an odd bible for a profession to choose because Jane Jacobs was profoundly suspicious of expertise, dismissive of professionals. She relied on observation and anecdote, not theory. It is a book trusting in street wisdom rather than the sophistication of academics and civil servants. Most of all, Jane told planners to get out of the way, a view that sat easily with the suspicion of elites, disdain for the governing class and distrust of top-down structures characteristic of the post-Vietnam, post-pill, post-pot, baby-boom consensus.

Jane Jacobs was no theorist. It is the emotion that flows through her work as much as the substance that has had a profound influence on the way we now think about cities. Two strands in particular. On the one hand, a profound respect for experience, for observation and for the wisdom of the citizen; the mother of schoolchildren, the local hardware store owner or the senior citizens on the bench in the park. If it did not make sense to them, it did not make sense. And the other, an infectious, often wicked sense of humor. If there is one mark of the great city, it is its humor. Jane told me once that her first job as a journalist was writing the agony column for the local Scranton newspaper. Since she had initiated the column, she was faced with the fundamental start-up problem of having no tortured souls to advise, so for a while she wrote both ends, coming and going, often giving herself hell in later letters for the poor advice she had offered in previous columns. She has had no shortage of advice since, both letters to and letters from; the characteristic tone of her work remained one of wry amusement in the ways of the city.

Jane Jacobs lived in my neighborhood—or, rather, I in hers—so we would bump into each other on Bloor Street, then a vibrantly diverse mix of butchers, bakers, bookstores, grocers, hardware stores and Hungarian restaurants. Hudson Street North. She developed a formidable persona in later years, a tall, big-boned woman given to great cape-like dresses, a triangle of white hair over a strong aquiline nose. With open sandals and those unforgettable glasses. The whole effect was somewhat bird-like, a big wise bird with the Scranton, Pennsylvania tones of an old crow. Formidable in all kinds of ways. Towards the end of her days, Jane would brandish a great curling ear trumpet, decorated in green paisley, swishing it around in front of each of her guests. Her increasingly acerbic opinions were similarly amplified.

For all she is revered as the patron saint of Toronto and its neighborhoods, Jane did not do "nice," Toronto's default demeanor. She was opinionated and argumentative, and if you got on the wrong side of her, that was it. We were once on a platform together at Boston College and I was making some erudite remarks she clearly thought rubbish. She interrupted me. "Joe, Joe, Joe." Her "bridge and tunnel" accent made it sound like jaw, jaw, jaw. "You're tawking nansense." The audience agreed.

I was followed on stage by an absurd academic who tried to use mathematical equations to scientifically prove or disprove the validity of Jacobs' hypotheses. If that wasn't enough, he made the fatal mistake of consistently addressing her as Professor Jacobs. "Staap calling me prafessa. I barely graduated high school," she barked. The academic and I slunk off stage together clutching our PowerPoints.

The rest of the world to this day thinks of Jane as a New Yorker, yet she lived in Toronto for almost forty years and has an almost tangible presence still, something with which every local city planner or city builder has to reckon. At the prime of her influence in the city, under the great mayoralty of David Crombie, she was the active inspiration behind the conception of the then-innovative St. Lawrence neighborhood in the east downtown, created under the direction of architect Alan Littlewood and planner Frank Lewinberg, groundbreaking in its day for its urban design, its mix of uses and its variety of affordable, market rental and ownership housing. It has since proven a resilient success. But by the 1980s and 1990s, an inevitable estrangement between her and City Hall took hold, along with the unhappy reduction of her text into Jane Jacobism, a mindset that entails reflexive hostility on behalf of the "community" to any major urban initiative. The radical transmuted to the reactionary. The local concern always trumped the larger view, with "progressives" finding in her work their justification for principled inaction.

It was unfortunate, and not an accurate representation of who she was. She certainly was not a lefty, despite moving in what were then predominantly left-wing circles in Toronto's Annex neighborhood. She fundamentally distrusted the state, preferring the energy of markets. She loved entrepreneurs, especially if they were not too big. If anything, she was a libertarian. Let good things happen and if the place is designed right, happen they will. Yet Jacobs' urban vision was ultimately grounded in and limited by the neighborhood. It provided no basis for large-scale intervention. And even at that neighborhood level her work seemed to support an impossible circularity. If what exists is good and can fix itself, why would you intervene? Who needs city planners?

* * *

Not surprisingly, as my generation of planners and city builders moved into the stage of life where we wanted, and were able, to do something substantial about our cities we found another guiding text: Robert Caro's *The Power Broker*. This biography of Jacobs' neighborhood-destroying/expressway-building foe from New York, Robert Moses, was published in 1974, just as a gang of us in Toronto City Hall were beginning to understand what it took to get something actually built in a big, complicated city. What was extraordinary about Caro's account of the master builder of post-war New York, still in print almost half a century later, was the fine detailing of the ways Robert Moses manipulated political power and public finance, the prerequisites for any major urban undertaking. Never elected to any office, he held numerous state and city positions, like New York State Parks Commissioner, New York City Planning Commissioner and, most importantly, Chairman of the Triborough Bridge and Tunnel Authority, whose revenues he skillfully diverted to finance his many projects. Caro's book is a remarkable achievement since he was unsympathetic to his subject, for good reason. Moses was a monomaniac and a bully whose many great parks, regeneration and transportation projects only barely tilt in the balance against the urban renewal and expressway manias that blighted his later years. Yet the achievements are undeniable—one million hectares of new parks in New York State, 658 playgrounds in New York City. Lincoln Center, the UN complex, the 1964 World's Fair and tens of thousands of affordable housing units that have mostly stood up well. And yes, nearly 5,000 kilometers of freeway and thirteen expressway bridges. The debate carries on to this day and the lines are still drawn. There have been several books on the Jacobs/Moses conflict and in recent years at least three recent exhibitions of his life and work. The two have been featured in both a play and an opera in New York in the past couple of years, further evidence of the drama and timelessness of their epic conflict.

Caro's book became for us a kind of devil's bible, an intensely practical manual to working the levers of urban power. He was particularly skilled in understanding how to finance city building, inherently an extremely expensive activity, and how to organize government to effectively deliver projects. He was in many ways the inventor of the public urban development companies that have played so important a role in contemporary big city urban regeneration. So while to most contemporary urbanists he was and is the devil incarnate, I was struck by how the New York engineers I later worked with revered him, what a formative figure he had been in their lives, certainly not the caricature that so many had drawn. For them, he was the man who made things happen, who had a vision for the city larger than the local city block. He understood and could harness the machine of the city with all the money, construction, business, investment and political power it required. And, despite the haranguing he has subsequently received, he was for much of his life motivated by a desire to improve the lot of the average New Yorker. He wanted to create clean, healthy new neighborhoods, each with its green play area. He wanted to get them to the many magnificent regional parks and beaches he built and to route them from their new urban and suburban neighborhoods to their jobs as quickly and conveniently as possible. Unfortunately for him, and fortunately for New York, the route ran right through Jane Jacobs' neighborhood.

Jane Jacobs was a critic, not a city builder, but any contemporary search for the perfect city has to start with her since she actually wrote it down, defining urban perfection for the past half century and more. Let's re-open that academic question. Is Jane Jacobs right about what makes the perfect city? It is useful to try and dig out Jacobs' core propositions. Happily, she could write a good sentence and capture complexity in a few words. Here is the essential Jane from *Death and Life:*

> . . . *lively, diverse, intense cities contain the seeds of their own regeneration, with energy enough to carry over for problems and needs outside themselves.*

Is she right? Heck of a question. A quick glance at any city can find plenty of examples that clearly confirm or contradict Jacobs' conclusions, unsurprisingly since cities are diverse complicated places. Jane clearly understates the importance of external economic and demographic forces in making the good city, in particular, the necessity of constant renewal by immigration rather than by an internal dynamic, as exemplified by Spadina Avenue's total change in ethnic character required for it to stay just the same. And most inner-city neighborhoods have found the energy for renewal not from internal seeds of regeneration but from those successive waves of immigrants, artists, gays, yuppies and empty-nesters who opened new businesses, demanded better schools and knew how to get city government to take better care of what was now their neighborhood. The revered locals were long gone, scooping up ridiculous cash for their homes and heading for the suburbs.

Jane also underestimated the power of broader market forces in shaping a street's retail make-up. Her beloved Bloor Street in the Annex is an example. Its former glorious diversity has been replaced by a continuous run of cheap restaurants catering to students from the neighboring University of Toronto. Similar changes have occurred on her revered Hudson Street in Greenwich Village, where the local retail lights have gone out. Transformational changes to the way people shop have called into doubt one of her essential engines of the good city, the local business on the street. Increasingly displaced by e-commerce and big-box price and selection competition, only restaurants and coffee shops are left to fill the voids. And there is a distinct limit to the linear footage of cappuccino/sushi/ramen any street can take. The pull of street theater seems only able to compete with price and convenience for quite limited markets. Without an ethnic, millennial or upper-income edge, most local retail streets in most cities in the developed world are having a grim time.

Her guidance, or lack thereof, for larger-scale city planning is another problem. She does not scale up easily. She does not provide the same direction—in fact, no direction—about what makes a city economically prosperous and functionally successful beyond the collective activity of the street and its local businesses. She says nothing about transit. She is suspicious of the roles of the great civic arts institutions, universities and hospitals, seeing them more as neighborhood breakers than prosperity makers. Her economy of cities does not encompass any of the big things a contemporary global city has to provide. Airports, high-quality education at all levels, cultural destinations, financial districts, convention centers, hospitals, tourism destinations, international institutions, transportation infrastructure. Frankly, I don't think she saw this basic equipment of the urban machine as important, so she gives no clues as to how a city should organize itself to provide it, other than "stay out of my 'hood and leave it be."

This has been an unfortunate legacy for many cities, but particularly for Toronto, whose small-town council has always regarded big projects as nuisances to be controlled and/or taxed rather than as key drivers of its success. It is the great paradox of Canada's leading global city that while its emergence as "the most livable city in the world" can in many ways be attributed to Jane Jacobs' influence, maintenance of this global standing, seemingly so unintentionally achieved, is going to require broader inspiration.

All the same, my work in new and old world cities from Hong Kong to Singapore, Manchester to Minneapolis, confirms Jacobs' emphasis on the street as the essential crucible of social order and economic activity in an urban setting. Doug Saunders' insightful analysis of immigrant cities in his book, *Arrival City*, brilliantly captures for the world's emerging cities how Jane Jacobs' principles promote the space for entrepreneurial activity and small business formation, critical processes in successful immigrant settlement. Jacobs was right about what makes a great street and neighborhood—just as well after decades of almost religious observance by city planners the world over. For the rest of the city, however, she provides very little help.

During the celebrations surrounding her 100th birthday, it became nonetheless clear that she had become Toronto's patron saint. Which is absolutely as it should be. She was not right on all things, and she was not without blemish, but who would want a saint who was? A saint without sin would defeat the purpose of saints. And there is another reason for her civic beatification. Jane Jacobs had unknowingly arrived at Toronto's pivot point. While the city had generated its own thinkers and writers of the stature of Northrop Frye and Marshall McLuhan, she was the first of global importance to move to Toronto from away, and stay. Great cities require, create and attract great people. When she first came to Toronto at the end of the sixties, she was asked by the U.S. press her impression of the city after having lived in Greenwich Village. Her response was classic Jane: "As a relatively recent transplant from New York, I am frequently asked whether I find Toronto sufficiently exciting. I find it almost too exciting. The suspense is scary. Here is the most hopeful and healthy city in North America, still unmangled, still with options."

One evening a few years before she died, I gave her a lift back from a dinner at architect Eb and his wife Jane Zeidler's house in Rosedale. She was recently widowed from her long-loved husband Bob, who had worked at Zeidler's practice, and she was having a bit of trouble moving around. We stashed her walker in the trunk and were almost back home to the Annex when, stopped at a traffic light, she leaned over.

"Jaw. Jaw. Tell me. Do you have any secret vices?"

Perhaps a bit of a come-hither look. Am I imagining that? It is a little-known fact, but the great urban thinker once made the pages of *Vogue*. During the war, she had modeled the "efficiency line," simple styles cut from a minimum of cloth, which was being rationed to outfit American troops. Anyone who has seen pictures of Jane from that time will know why she made the magazine, for which she also wrote. In the back jacket photo of the Random House classic edition of *The Death and Life of Great American Cities* she is crossing a serious pair of legs over a Greenwich Village barstool. She was a striking woman in her prime.

She leaned a little closer to my ear. "Cos I do."

Pause. Hands on the wheel.

"I really, really, like to smoke. These people, ya know. These people who look after me [she was at that point surrounded by caregivers], they don't approve." There was Scranton disdain in her voice. "They never let me get out to buy any."

With relief, I nipped out to the corner store and got her a couple of packs. Benson and Hedges Menthol. She cleverly concealed them about her person. That is my last memory of Jane, leaving her on the porch of her Annex home, as she turned to nod goodbye with a look of almost teenage complicity. Jane could spot an enabling sap.

* * *

Everyone in Toronto has their favorite Spadina Avenue Chinese restaurant. Mine is *Xam Yu*. Plastic tablecloths, fish-tank Chinese, with huge steamed Pacific oysters in ginger and mussels in black-bean sauce. Remarkably inexpensive lobster. Big fat clams in the shell. Abalone. It is where we would go as a family for weekend lunches. In mid-winter, the doors would let in an ocean of cold from the knees down. It did not seem to bother the kids who, when bored with adult conversation, would make a camp under the plastic table covers, tying the grown-up's shoelaces together as we chatted above. It is up the street from my office, so now I tend to go there with business colleagues, or when I get that seafood urge.

It is a restaurant of which Jane Jacobs would have approved. Family run, small, neighborly. Part of an eco-system of Chinese and Vietnamese restaurants and big wholesale food merchants on the street. But I can't help noticing that there are fewer and fewer such businesses, and even *Xam Yu* looks as if it might not be here for long. This part of the street is looking tired. About a third of the storefronts are effectively vacant. Familiar places are slipping away. The refresh is of an utterly different character, and the Chinese are now increasingly transforming the suburbs, not the central city, "creative class" industries like ours are crowding up from the south, university-fueled gentrification pushes down from the north, and the ever-changing Kensington Market district immediately west is going through yet another transformation into something—not quite sure what. My guess is that in a couple more decades the Asian presence on the street will have all but disappeared, a half-century after it arrived.

Big, external urban forces are fueling these transformations, not the creative energy of the street itself. The street is merely the stage. Above all, two forces: first, the extraordinary economic energy unleashed by Toronto's rise up the global city rankings; second, the continuing refresh of consistently high levels of quality immigration. The seeds of regeneration are not local, they are blown in from afar, although they need this healthy urban soil to flourish. These forces demonstrate how Jane can only take us so far. Certainly, at this stage in its development, Toronto needs a different kind of instruction. In our obsessive concern for home, we have neglected the machine. Toronto has big deficits in transit, housing, economic development and connectivity. But as importantly, it needs to stop thinking of itself as a village. It needs a confident vision of itself as a global city. The truth is Jane Jacobs cannot help us with that. So, it is time to leave her streets, leave Spadina, leave Toronto, and go back to where Jane came from, to the city in which I have spent much of my professional life—New York.

3

NEW YORK CITY –
TOP OF THE SPIKE

New York was my first big city. Even today, decades later, flying down the approach along the Hudson, I am dazzled, Manhattan laid out like a vast ocean liner afloat in shining morning rivers and seas. Has there ever been a more beautiful human artifact than this? New York, New York. Top of the spike.

Why New York? Why is its future so important to the future of cities? Because from its unique position at the top of the global urban hierarchy, it projects the trajectory of all big cities. New York came to dominance at the end of the nineteenth century, consolidating its business position with a dramatic expansion of its transit system, the construction of transformative bridges and utility infrastructure, all while welcoming hundreds of thousands of new citizens from around the world. It continued to build with force and competence even through the depression and World War II, adding signature development projects and expressways, and aggressively embracing urban renewal. That era of city building was halted by the cultural changes of the 1960s and 1970s, a shift to localism so ably articulated by Jane Jacobs, as well as by changes to the manufacturing economy and the explosion of automobile use. Older industrial districts were abandoned, containerization rendered the city's traditional port functions redundant, and hordes of people moved out to the suburbs. These were the *Bladerunner* years. Then, two decades later, the same powerful economic forces that had stranded the city began to move in its favor. The rise of the financial services sector, the growth of media industries, the increasing attraction of urban tourism all helped to recharge the city. The crime rate dropped, at first slowly and then precipitously. Population and wealth surged. The city's renewed strength was exemplified by its rapid response to two life-threatening events in one decade, 9/11 and the 2008 crash of Wall Street. The New York that emerged from these calamities was even stronger and more capable than before.

Our business first arrived in New York as part of the crew of staff and consultants hired by the Toronto developer Olympia and York to realize its first big international project, World Financial Center (now named Brookfield Place). It sits at the heart of Battery Park City, a large-scale new urban district along the Hudson River in Lower Manhattan. There was almost a dozen of us hired hands from Toronto in and around O&Y during its dizzying rise. Paul Reichmann, the firm's prime mover, described us as his "toolbox." I guess that is what we were. He found the money and the tenants; we did everything else. Working for O&Y around the world was the start of my professional life. They were for one wonderful decade the world stars of high-quality, large-scale urban development. Every city wanted them. They only engaged at the top, with mayors, ministers, high-level bureaucrats, the best engineers and architects. Those of us in the toolbox gained experience and global contacts that we milked for the rest of our professional lives, long after O&Y came crashing down and sent us all scrambling.

We were a close team. We had all worked together at Toronto City Hall in the 1970s under Mayor David Crombie, creating a new plan for downtown Toronto, a pivotal stage in the city center's remarkable transformation from a dull, single-use commercial district surrounded by parking lots to the explosion of housing, retail, culture and street life that it is today. All great projects produce such a team—you can see them in the planning and development culture of any successful city, a dense network of people who went through the fire together to produce something good. As a result, these people trust each other when, years later, one of the tribe picks up the phone.

The Reichmann's were my most remarkable clients, an orthodox Jewish family, deeply religious, running a ground-breaking business that was a bizarre combination of global enterprise and corner store. Or maybe it was just a real-world *schul.* You could never be sure. In the late 1980s, they essentially poached anyone they fancied in the City of Toronto Housing and Planning Departments and shipped us off, first to New York and then to London. They had met us, the City Hall staffers, while developing their first big Toronto building, First Canadian Place. What they saw in us is hard to say, but perhaps a Canadian modesty, a politeness, a professional practicality that somehow fit with their distinctly old-world business culture. For a few glorious years that culture seemed to work. Certainly, neither New Yorkers nor, later, Londoners, in the Canary Wharf years, really knew quite what to make of these quiet Canadians, nor of the formal, observant, soft-spoken Reichmanns. *"Youall gotta paper bags on ya heads"* was the way one Brookalino in the New York office described us. Whatever that meant, it was probably accurate, and it might have been one of the reasons for our success.

Battery Park City had been vacant for years after a succession of failed redevelopment attempts. There we helped build the first large-scale urban development in New York to reflect the Jane Jacobs consensus of how a city should be designed. Like Toronto's St. Lawrence project on which many of us had worked, it attempted to recreate on a blank site the texture and liveliness characteristic of the parts of cities we loved. A simple grid of streets, buildings designed in groups, with a concentration of stores and restaurants along a spine avenue. Jane would have been proud. Yet it was remarkable how much regulation and control, what precise zoning and design guidance, were necessary to achieve the random variety of a typical New York district.

Our job was to try and stitch into the heart of this new district something of much larger scale, a massive new office complex to provide the energy, employment and revenues necessary to animate the neighborhood and to pay for its public spaces, the essential machine in the heart of home. What really makes Battery Park City a success today is the way that urban energy combines with the quality of those parks and the extended esplanade beside the Hudson. An utter delight, made with the permanence of a big city. There is a real attention to detail, to the quality of materials, with an urban substance and confidence that is missing in so much contemporary city design. The public art collection displayed throughout the neighborhood is exemplary, an outdoor gallery of the best of New York's modernist traditions. A simple focus on form and beauty and, with the exception of the appallingly literal Irish immigration memorial, none of the diversions of identity correctness—or, worse, irony—that turn most cities' public art installations into cheap one-liners. Lucky is the city like New York that knows art.

Nothing good in a city happens unless one individual makes it so. The reason the places and spaces of Battery Park City are of such quality is because of one remarkable person: Amanda Burden. When I had first come to New York in the seventies, Burden and her then-husband Carter were the city's "it" couple, on the cover of every magazine—as close as the U.S. can come to aristocrats, one a Paley, the other a Vanderbilt. But rather than live the life of a socialite, Burden went back to school, training at Columbia as a city planner, later becoming what we *sotto voce* called the "vice-president of good taste" for the agency responsible for Battery Park City. Great taste she had. And an attention to detail. We would see her at her lunch break sneaking out with a pair of secateurs to dead-head the roses or trim some shrubs or fix something else that had caught her discerning eye. Great cities are made by great people, and Amanda Burden went on to become one of the world's great city planners as Commissioner under Mayor Michael Bloomberg. And without a doubt, her clear, elegant energy established her as an early role model for women in such positions the world over.

As Commissioner, Burden demonstrated a great strategic sense in addition to her attention to detail. As the leading global city, New York is still the effective center of the global economy and thus one of the most sought-after places in the world to live and do business. Like each of the top dozen global cities, it is growing rapidly and running out of space, a problem compounded by the city's unique geography, with the densely developed island of Manhattan surrounded by less thriving, lower-density boroughs. To help solve the city's problems of increasingly unaffordable housing, lack of large-scale opportunities for development and the relative inaccessibility of the boroughs, Bloomberg's team set about rezoning the extensive, unseen resource of empty industrial backlands and abandoned ports that lined the city's river edges. That action, which had defeated generations of planners, required foraging through dense layers of land-use regulation, the Gordian knots of zoning and environmental legislation that are the legacy of every special interest and good intention in any city, although New York's are probably thicker and more resistant to change than most. Burden's determination paid off, resulting in the incremental rezoning of 40 per cent of the city, creating over a million square feet of newly buildable space and preserving or creating 165,000 housing units, providing and maintaining affordable housing for about 500,000 people. Burden would always say that she wanted to be a city builder in the style of Jane Jacobs, but with the scale of Robert Moses. The results speak for themselves.

* * *

If you wanted to understand Bloomberg, arguably the best mayor of any world city in recent times, you just had to go to his City Hall. I had visited frequently during the Koch and Dinkins administrations, trying to get approvals for O&Y's projects. From the outside, City Hall is a charming, diminutive French Provincial bandbox of a building, a wonderful frivolity at the heart of Lower Manhattan. But on the inside it was a complete mess of corridors and cubicles, dingy spaces and barely functioning office systems. Add to that the post-9/11 security imperatives and you had a building that approached functional failure.

Bloomberg came to the mayoralty from the great open trading floors of Wall Street, huge un-encumbered spaces packed with people in close contact, supported by the best equipment the financial services industry could buy. How he redesigned the workspaces of the old City Hall speaks volumes about his strategy for city management. He gave up the office occupied by generations of New York mayors, with George Washington's desk and wonderful views over City Hall Square, and installed himself instead in a former hearing room about the size of a high school gymnasium. In that large open space with no walls and no distinctions as to rank or privilege, he was surrounded by his deputy mayors and about 100 senior and support staff. Bloomberg's office was right at the center, a small half-height carrel consisting of a desk and two screens, shared with his secretary. Perhaps thirty square feet for the head of the world's leading city. That proximity replaced the need for lots of formal meetings since the people you wanted to meet were right next to you. All the former executive offices were turned into common rooms with glass walls. Everyone could see what was going on, a practical expression of transparency and the Mayor had to walk by half his senior staff to get to his desk or go to the bathroom.

Bloomberg, elected for three terms, was a self-made billionaire who stood on a platform of re-inventing city government. He is one of the few who has actually done it. New York City employs some 300,000 people and commands a budget the size of a small country. His greatest achievement was to generate a sense of excitement and possibility within that bureaucracy, attracting an impressive cadre of remarkable deputy mayors with proven resumes in the outside world, each with responsibility for a different city function, along with a staff of energetic, bright young talent. One thing is common to all great cities: all the hard work is done by people in their thirties who must then be pushed into positions of power and influence quickly, later to be re-invigorated by a rush of fresh talent. How do you draw on and inspire that talent? By getting a smile or a nod hello from the Mayor on your way to the snack table. Bloomberg, a healthy eater, was so disgusted by the standard City Hall fare that he himself paid for a new "snacks and fruit juices bar" right in the room. The energy of his nod would keep most thirty-somethings fueled for a month.

Skeptical, I asked a colleague whether this was all for show. How much time did Bloomberg actually spend in the center of the bullpen, as it was known? "About a third of his time," came the response. Remarkable.

No less impressive than Bloomberg were the people with whom he surrounded himself. Joel Klein, the high-flying former White House counsel who became his School Chancellor, with a mandate to transform the city's school system. Janet Sadiq-Khan, his visionary Commissioner of Transportation, whose clever, imaginative creation of a generous bike lane system and instant parks have transformed the street life of the city. Dan Doctoroff, who had previously led a large private equity investment firm and fronted NYC2012, New York's Olympic bid, was Deputy Mayor for economic development and possibly the smartest, most effective city builder I have ever encountered. He and all his new colleagues were people with substantial achievements outside of City Hall before Bloomberg brought them in. One of the difficulties in most cities is that they lack effective ways of refreshing their staff, especially those with a hard-baked civil service system. Certainly, few cities have ever assembled the quality and depth of team that Bloomberg deployed in his bullpen. And it showed in a series of bold, transformative initiatives.

Bloomberg's remarkable strategic direction for the future of his city is best exemplified by the story of Cornell Tech, a science university and innovation district he instigated on Roosevelt Island in the East River. The city for which he became responsible upon taking office in 2002 was still severely wounded by the events of 9/11. Although still the capital of the world, its economy was in his view far too narrowly focused on a few sectors—most obviously financial services, media and fashion—and on being the high-end neighborhood for the world's super rich, something that was making it increasingly difficult to accommodate the innovative thirty-somethings critical for the new economy. That new economy was being created everywhere but in New York City, primarily in Silicon Valley, up the Pacific coast, and in Boston. Bloomberg forced his team to take a hard-eyed view of the city's competitive advantages and shortcomings. Incredible as it is for outsiders to believe, he mused openly about New York ceasing to be world class. His team produced an analysis of all the city's competitors: San Francisco, for its university-driven tech sector and ability to offer a compelling lifestyle; London, New York's only challenger at the top of the spike, with the only comparable culture and a burgeoning tech sector of its own. The mayor's people looked jealously at London's ability to secure and implement an imaginative, successful Olympic Games—Doctoroff's bid for New York had failed to get close. And Singapore, exemplifying the Asian world coming on at speed, to say nothing of Shanghai and Hong Kong. New York's position at the top of the spike was by no means assured.

Bloomberg, the businessman, understood. He had to add to the city's structural economic power. If the city did not already have the requisite university, despite protests to the contrary from Columbia and New York University, it had better buy one. In 2010, he issued an invitation for the world's leading universities to establish a science campus in New York, offering a choice of sites along the East River and $100-million as start-up capital. Strong bidding ensued from universities all over the world. The winning proposal came from Cornell University and its partner, the Technion-Israel Institute of Technology. All respondents identified Roosevelt Island as the optimal location, for good reason. Located right opposite the United Nations, under Paul Simon's lyric 59th Street Bridge, it would become the most visible manifestation of Bloomberg's new city.

The first elements of what will ultimately be a $2-billion complex consisting of a beautifully designed, environmentally state-of-the-art university campus, residences and an innovation/commercialization center opened in 2017, just seven years after the initial concept was offered to the world. That is warp speed in the world of city building. The scheme has also attracted remarkably generous philanthropic donations, with over half a billion dollars already pledged. I cannot think of a better example of capable city leadership than this: thinking strategically, acting creatively, searching globally, delivering with excellence, all in record time. The city's brain, heart, wallet and arm all connected as they should be, acting with speed and purpose. And as a testament to the power of competitive urban shaming, both Columbia and NYU have themselves initiated rival high-tech innovation machines.

On the other side of Manhattan from Cornell Tech, a dense cluster of new buildings is beginning to shoot out of the ground on the Hudson

River. Hudson Yards is the other great Bloomberg/Doctoroff development legacy to New York City, the largest and certainly the most
ambitious urban development in the United States today. The twenty-
eight-acre west side site, located in the mid-thirties, will eventually
accommodate at least sixteen skyscrapers and have a total floor area
of around sixteen-million square feet, about double that of London's
Canary Wharf on which it is in some ways modeled. To speak of a "site"
is something of a misnomer. Beneath Hudson Yards is one of the most
heavily used rail corridors and train storage areas in the world, requiring
the construction of a massive bridging deck on which the new buildings are actually set. The rail yards were the reason the area had eluded
generations of developers and grand schemes. One of the most unprepossessing parts of Manhattan, just south of the fabled Hell's Kitchen,
it had become an urban junkyard of open tracks, tunnel entrances,
sanitation buildings, storage yards and a human landscape of struggle
and despair. Dan Doctoroff finally figured out how to cut through
the tangles of jurisdictional complexity and impossible engineering
problems and to invent a financial model to make redevelopment possible. Doctoroff formulated a complex physical plan combined with
a sophisticated set of public financing tools and private development
incentives that used the increase in land and property tax values, along
with the sale of bonus development rights, to fund an extension of
the subway to the development and to pay for the ambitious series
of public parks proposed for the scheme. He was re-inventing half a
century later the techniques of Robert Moses.

It is rarely some fatal flaw or clear impediment that kills such ambitious urban proposals. It is typically a slow death from the collective
choke of bureaucratic delay, the dense weight of regulation, the endless complications of financing, ownership and property rights, the
lazy eye-blink of political attention. This is what in the U.K. is called
"the blob," the secret government of every city that, left to itself, will
smother any creative initiative. To defeat the blob is the most challenging of urban tasks. It requires stamina and guile, and someone who
regularly wakes up in the middle of the night knowing that it is only
he or she who can prevail.

* * *

If the adjective Bloombergian could be applied to only two projects, Hudson Yards and Cornell Tech would be the appropriate recipients. Hudson Yards is unashamedly neo-liberal, a wealth-creating machine for metropolitan corporations and their managerial class, executed at scale, focusing extensive public resources on the glittering transformation of a district whose once gritty, if overstated, authenticity is gone forever. In contrast, Cornell Tech understands that the urban machine is ultimately fueled by brains and that it must have the best factory for their production. Both projects understand, embrace and augment the necessary power of the machine; both excite with delight.

Cornell Tech is now springing from the prow of Roosevelt Island. Just down river is another island, Governors Island, one of the most intriguing places in any global city. Governors Island has for decades, centuries even, been the sleeping beauty of New York, a former coast-guard and military base in the middle of New York harbor less than a kilometer from both Manhattan and Brooklyn. A place so near yet so far that few New Yorkers have ever been there, or even really noticed it as they steamed by on the Staten Island ferry. The island has a long history, from being a seventeenth-century Dutch settlement to the home of the British colonial governor and then a staging post in the Revolutionary War, a harbor defense in the War of 1812, finally a training base, barracks, airfield and military jail. Each stage has left its mark, resulting in a glorious array of heritage buildings of every kind: forts, bastions, mansions, dormitory blocks, houses of all kinds, hospitals, schools, churches, cinemas and bowling alleys. No cars, no vehicles, no ambient noise but the water and the trees, all on an island at the center of the world. And no people. Full year-round general public access is still not available and a permanent residential presence is prohibited. Fifty-nine nationally registered historic buildings, the vast majority of them empty, sit under a wonderful canopy of mature trees, with views out to the towers of Manhattan and the Brooklyn Bridge. Just across the water, close enough to shake her hand, is the Statue of Liberty. A long-born island of almost virginal beauty, a mermaid in the metropolis.

I worked for Dan Doctoroff and for the island's then-new boss Leslie Koch on plans for its transformation. The difficulty of trying to plan Governors Island, as Leslie Koch soon learned when she took it over, is just that extraordinary uniqueness, that extreme paradox. It was a time machine, defiant of urban gravity, a black hole of peace and calm in the heart of the city. It was too easy to be charmed by the isle. I know I was.

Koch, who began her career with Microsoft just as the company was starting, was running an educational trust in New York when she got a call from Bloomberg's office asking her to head up Governors Island. "There's an island in the harbor, would you like to run it?" She did not know the mayor. He had simply identified the talent he needed and put in the call. She insisted on a meeting before taking the post, to which he grudgingly agreed. She asked the question, "What do you want me to do?" She got the good city executive's only answer: "If I knew what to do, I wouldn't have asked you." As she was leaving the meeting he stopped her and said, "By the way. You get two strikes."

Koch knew her first task was to move people across the harbor from Manhattan and Brooklyn to Governors Island. The ancient ferries that then served the island were unable to meet the demand for the events and activities she had in mind, let alone convey the thousands of workers and support activities that could result from the permanent occupation of the almost two-million square feet of heritage buildings. She bought a high capacity ferry from Woods Hole, Massachusetts, that proved to be in such poor shape it was sold for scrap at a loss of nearly $900,000. One strike left.

Her strategy was to play both short and long games. In the short term, she dramatically increased the number and range of events and amenities on the island. Concerts, hammocks, kayaks, art, food and antique fairs, film shoots—anything that would get people out to the site, so they could be charmed too. It worked. Summer open attendance shot up from 20,000 a year to almost half a million. The island became part of the active mental map of the city for the first time in its history. The longer game was more difficult. After a global competition, she retained the landscape architecture firm of West 8 from the Netherlands, renowned for their imaginative, quirky work, to transform the now cleared southern half of the island. Their dramatic topography of winding paths leading to a canyon-cut mountain finally opened to great applause in the summer of 2016.

Koch had less success finding long-term occupants to re-occupy the heritage buildings, let alone developers for the substantial vacant parcels on either side of the southern half of the island. A few buildings were filled. The New York Harbor School is a high school occupying the former military hospital building. It features an academic program related to New York's maritime experience and is part of a larger project of re-inventing educational delivery in the city, supported by both private and public funding. The lobby of the school is unlike any other I have entered, with a long aquarium featuring the full range of aquatic life found in the harbor. Each entry class seeds a bed of oysters. Sadly, they cannot yet eat them upon graduation but the students have helped to restore what was for the long life of the harbor its most prolific food source. The oysters are also working to cure the condition that once rendered them unsafe: their extraordinary filtering ability, up to 200 liters of water a day, is cleaning the harbor habitat. I cannot think of a better life lesson for high school students. Bloomberg set a unique mayoral target of bedding a billion oysters in the harbor. My kind of electoral program.

Our firm's later work on Governors Island was to help the city find long-term users of the remaining buildings and developers for the large sites on the south side of the island. While it sounds simple, it is not. How do you draw investment to an island that is built but empty, close but inaccessible, urban but rural, simultaneously big and small, lacking adequate sewer, water, gas and digital services, shops, cafés and restaurants? It has nothing but trees and history, water and beauty. It is a reminder that glorious heritage and landscape and are not in themselves sufficient. Yet the island will eventually be occupied. Great cities abhor a vacuum, and the availability of large, flexible sites and an extraordinary range of heritage structures will benefit from the new economic activity exploding along the East River in Brooklyn and Queens, sparked by Cornell Tech. The idea of extending the subway under the island and on to Brooklyn's Red Hook has now been put on the table by both the mayor and governor of New York. That will do it.

* * *

Nobody knows New York if Manhattan's all you know. "Uptown and The Bronx" it says on the platform—was there ever a more resonant urban poem? We are going up the IRT to Manhattan's complete opposite. We are going to the library.

Getting off the 5 train at Simpson Street is an urbanist's education. This is the other world of New York, home of the precariat, where the informal labor markets of the global south land in the big city. A beautiful station, one of those important reminders of how much a previous generation of transit engineers loved New York. Elevated over the street, platforms with cream-colored windscreens and red canopy roofs, the stairs in strong steel frames with ornamented green fences and lampposts. Underneath the platform, everything is being sold: food, knick-knacks, cheap clothing, whatever else you need. All with a benign buzz, mocking my lingering "Burn, Baby, Burn" image of the Bronx. But never forget just what a segregated city New York is—and the minefields for politicians in negotiating its contested territories.

I have an old leftie friend, one of the Toronto City Hall/O&Y team, who subsequently made a shed-load of money in real estate and put some into a bunch of restaurants in Manhattan, now employing all together over a hundred people. In the face of the Trump election, the old leftie in him revived and he determined he was going to do what he could to help regularize the immigration status of those of his employees he suspected, despite their all having an apparently valid Social Security Number, might not be fully legal. He got no uptake at all. A long-time kitchen captain explained to him that every single one of them was undocumented. All were scared to raise their heads. They had bought their SSNs in a bodega in the Bronx, or in Bensonhurst or Flushing, somewhere out at the ends of the subway lines. All were regularly paying their deductions but to the benefit of who knew? The geographic distance from the Simpson Street station to Manhattan is only a few miles; the socio-economic gap is as broad as it can be.

I am in the Bronx to visit Colbert Nembhard, Chief Librarian of the Morrisania Public Library. It is a bit of a walk from the Simpson Street station but on a sunny day the South Bronx is a pleasure. It looks prosperous, a middle-class black neighborhood. Well-kept houses and apartments, some signs of new investment but no hipster gentrification. That is happening, but in the South Bronx, half a dozen stations south from here. The library is a building of municipal substance with a brick façade, deep-set windows, a limestone portico and boundary wall, and interiors of dark wood. It was built in 1908, about the same time as the station, when the Bronx was the newly developed home for waves of mostly Eastern European, strongly Jewish immigration. It was the place to which you moved your family from the Lower East Side. A few decades later, it became the place to which you moved from Harlem.

If there ever could be a hero of public libraries, Colbert would be it. He is a quiet, gentle, unassuming man but his commitment and innovation are increasingly well known. *The New York Times* had a long piece on him in 2016. Lester Holt interviewed him on the NBC Nightly News. He came to the U.S. from Jamaica as a teenager in 1975. His first job as a library trainee was at Morrisania and he came back in 1991 as manager and has been there ever since. For him, the library is the stable, quiet heart of the community, the freely available connection to learning and the world. That is evident not only inside the building, full of people with a remarkable diversity of age and ethnicity, everyone working away, but also outside in the widest reaches of the community. Every week he personally takes his quality literacy programs to homeless shelters, giving the youngest of children an early experience of learning without which they might be lost when they start school. Digital equity is his other big campaign. You can see the results in all the kids and grown men and women focused on the library's screens. He knows how these people live, how little money, time and quiet there is at home, how whatever digital connections they might have will be fought over. The library is clean and orderly.

Colbert knows how to negotiate that tricky line that makes a library welcoming, yet lets no one individual mess it up for the others.

His two decades at the library have given Colbert a unique perspective on the community's evolution. The once African-American majority was first joined by Hispanics and more recently by West Africans and a sizable Haitian minority. The library system underpins the processes of immigrant settlement by providing immediate access to the world through its free computers, and by supporting ID-NYC, a city-sponsored program of identity cards for the undocumented. Colbert tells me that the library system is so concerned about the threats leveled by the Trump administration at new immigrants that all the source identity info provided to get a New York ID is being burned by the city as part of its "sanctuary city" program. Like the districts at the end of the subway lines we will visit in other cities, the Bronx is making itself a home to those fleeing the chaos of so much of the world.

A regular at the local Planning Board 3, Colbert tries to link the library with good planning and land use, and he has the smarts to squeeze community investment from developers. He is the neighborhood broker, making connections with the police and community services, leveraging more affordable housing, supporting the neighborhood "greening" initiatives and putting the library at the forefront of community activism. He has even tapped into metropolitan wealth. The Durst family, major generational builders in New York, are now directing serious philanthropy to the Morrisania. Perhaps that New York wealth and power appreciate that its future depends as much on what happens among the newcomers in Morrisania as on the innovations of Cornell Tech or the capitalism of Hudson Yards.

Colbert and I sit together in little kids chairs and talk. With his bright eyes and cheerful laugh, he is a pleasure to be around. He is a man of faith and talks about his church. How fine, in a country of increasingly bombastic Christianity, to see what the real thing looks like.

* * *

I looked for a place to eat in Morrisania. Lots of interesting places to be sure, but my old reflexive white guy hesitation prevails and I headed back down the 5 train to Grand Central Station. To the Oyster Bar, for old time's sake. During my years of commuting to New York, O&Y's office was on Park Avenue just up the street from Grand Central. The Oyster Bar was my refuge, a place of respite in the basement of what was then a grimy station, dank with urine, shadowy figures slinking around its hidden corners like a Batman movie. It is now glowingly restored, the finest transportation terminal in the world, and the Oyster Bar retains that same comforting metropolitan buzz. It is a restaurant where the servers don't give a shit and you had better know what you want and quick. They are the lords of their horseshoe bar, taking orders fast like an old-fashioned stock exchange, cooking with effortless sleight of hand on their steam-sleeved swivel pots. It is worth the trip. Is there any ambrosia in the world equivalent to their oyster pan roast? A recipe as old as New York.

The tiled caverns of the Oyster Bar convey that unique sense of permanence and renewal of any great city. New York is the essential test bed for the forces fashioning the perfect city. Every metropolis in the world echoes its confusion over where and how to promote redevelopment, over who benefits, over how to attract the new economy and how to cope with the torrent of rootless global wealth pouring in and engendering striking economic inequality. Also echoed are its struggles with immigration, settlement and racial tension. Every great city is wrestling with the competing demands of feeding the machine while not overwhelming home. Moses and Jacobs still hover over this debate, the consummate New York power broker and his Greenwich Village nemesis arguing about top-down and bottom-up, about whose approach can complete the journey to the perfect city. It is time for some fresh air in this debate—time for a city with great street cooking that has found its own unique way to global prominence. We are off to Singapore.

4

SINGAPORE –
THE OTHER WAY TO
BUILD A CITY

The approach to Singapore's Changi Airport explains the city's existence. To the west, the Straits of Malacca lead to the Indian Ocean. To the east lie the South China Sea and the Pacific Ocean. Below stretches the ten-kilometer-wide Singapore Strait, one of the busiest sea highways in the world. It is Panama or Suez without the canals, one of the key strategic routes on the planet.

The drive in from Changi Airport has to be the loveliest airport-to-city approach in the world. The broad boulevard runs for twenty kilometers and is over-arched by huge flowering trees, with a trim hedge of bougainvillea on the center median. Traffic flows easily and you get glimpses of the bay. Your arrival in the city is sending you a message: they do things differently in Singapore. Lee Kuan Yew, legendary creator of the modern Singapore, personally selected the trees.

Singapore is an island state, a one-tier government right on the equator. It is about the same geographic size as the City of Toronto but, at 5.4 million residents, it has double the population. Founded as a British colony in 1819, it achieved independence in the early 1960s, first as part of the Malaysia Federation, then separating in 1965 to form a unique city-state. Under Lee Kuan Yew's forceful tutelage, it established a distinctive style of government, propelling it in half a century from widespread poverty to one of the wealthiest countries/cities in the world.

A number of world cities have achieved elements of perfection in how they design and manage themselves. Copenhagen in its bicycle friendliness, Stockholm in its practical environmentalism, Bilbao with its cultural leap, Portland with its transit system, Paris with its *grands projets*. Singapore has as much to teach and more, although understanding the dynamics of its success requires a deep intake of breath.

Let's start with that lovely, easy drive from the airport. There is remarkably little congestion in Singapore because the island has mounted the most comprehensive "war on the car" of any global city. To buy a car you must first obtain a certificate of entitlement. There are only half a million cars in Singapore for a population of six-million people, one of the lowest rates of car ownership in the world. The government releases only enough new certificates to allow a 1 per cent annual increase in the number of cars. (Even that rate, it recently announced, will be dropping, replacing only the number deregistered each year). You have to bid to get a certificate and the going rate tops $75,000. It is only good for ten years. On top of this, you need to buy the car, which is loaded with import duties, and then you pay some of the stiffest road tolls in the world. As partial compensation, the city's roads are largely empty. Most people use Singapore's superb, modern, inexpensive and ever-expanding transit system. Nothing could be more different from the deliberately cheap gas and car subsidies of the new Gulf city-states of Dubai, Abu Dhabi and Qatar and the dispiriting, bombastic and dysfunctional urban environments those strategies have created. Singapore has got it perfect, but it is not for the faint-hearted urban manager.

This strongly directed way of doing things is reflected throughout the city. An extraordinary 90 per cent of residents own their homes but, more remarkably, 83 per cent live in public housing. This program of public-housing ownership, as opposed to rental, is advanced through clever support programs to households of all incomes. Lee Kuan Yew felt people had to own something to look after it, to become committed citizens, and to amass the capital with which to start a business. The sales office of the Housing Development Board (HDB), Singapore's public housing agency, reflects that perspective. The huge, high-ceilinged showroom feels like a luxury car dealership. There is an immaculate selection of model suites and attentive customer service staff. I have never seen anything less like the typical public housing office. HDB sells only to locals. The private market, in which prices have now reached absurdly high levels, is for foreigners and the super-rich. This split between public and private markets takes the speculative pressure off the dominant housing supply, simultaneously securing local housing needs while dealing with international demands.

The housing estates are high rise, high density and highly sought after. They break all of Jane Jacobs' prescriptions for successful community design, with relentless mega-blocks, terrible street relationships, and all kinds of unsurveillable spaces. Yet, so far, it would seem to have engendered none of the undesirable social behavior one might expect. Singapore's physical form destroys any theory of urban-design determinism, an important reminder that badly designed buildings and poorly conceived urban spaces do not directly cause anti-social behavior. People can do that all on their own. And Singapore, for better or worse, has created a culture in which people do not behave badly.

Our work with the HDB is nevertheless concerned with what might be described as correcting a Jane Jacobs deficit. We are always trying to find ways of replanning or adding to these estates, inserting more active streets and places for small business formation, informal gathering spaces. We try to achieve similar densities but in a more community-friendly and entrepreneurial-friendly form. In our recent project, the expansion of what is almost a completely new town called Punggol at the edge of the main built-up area, we have doubled or tripled the tightness of the street grid, to increase the amount of frontage, the number of corners, and the opportunities for retail and business. That new closeness is relieved with new parks and open space corridors and a celebration of some of the island's earliest housing clusters. In true Singaporean fashion, it is almost completely built in just a few years.

Singapore is a great client, but you have to be careful what you suggest, as they move with unsettling speed. Put an idea on a plan and in a blink people are moving in. They want urgently to increase their population to seven million over the next twenty years to service their burgeoning economy. They fear that if they fail to build good new housing, they will create the slums or squatter communities characteristic of most growing cities. It is another aspect of Singapore that continually strikes you: the fluid, effective connection between the brain, the wallet and the hand; the sheer urban competence. The civil service is well trained. All of them appear to have spent time at the world's best universities. They are among the best paid civil servants in the world. They are also empowered, which has its ups and downs. It is expected that they will deliver and that they will be dismissed if they do not. The country is ranked among the least corrupt in the world. Could that be the reason?

The Singaporean difference is most evident in social policy. There is none of the government-provided pensions, welfare, housing benefits, health care or unemployment insurance programs characteristic of developed nations. Instead, the country has the lowest rate of income tax in the world and citizens are required to save 20 per cent of their incomes in a government-managed Central Provident Fund, to which employers make a matching 17 per cent contribution. Contributors own their assets in the fund, although withdrawals during their working life are limited to health expenditures, mortgage payments and educational expenses. This provident fund, in turn, provides a large government-controlled capital resource from which to finance infrastructure investment. The outcomes are astonishing. Take health care: Singapore has one of the best health care systems in the world yet one that consumes only 5 per cent of GDP, in contrast to around 10 per cent in most Western countries and, of course, 17 per cent in the U.S., which, incidentally, registers far worse health outcomes. How is that done? By combining the equity of a universal access system with the efficiency of privatized delivery and by incentivizing personal responsibility for maintaining good health. That is perfect.

The social contract is the complete opposite of that in the west. Singapore has very low rates of taxation, which means you do not get much directly from the government but it helps you look after yourself. You are expected to work, which means the country has an unemployment rate of 2 per cent and is not burdened with heavy income transfer obligations. Lee Kuan Yew hated welfare programs. In his mind, they blunted ambition and bankrupted the state.

They do other things differently in Singapore, things that are harder to take. Homosexuality is technically illegal, as in much of Asia, although the law is unenforced. First offences for drug use and public drunkenness can be punished by caning. Drug traffickers can be hanged. By Western cultural standards, this is an impossibly tough approach to crime, although it clearly has consequences. The country has one of the lowest rates of drug use in the world and since the majority of urban crime in cities the world over is related to substance abuse, the removal of so primary a cause has palpable consequences for the city's livability. That is why all that poorly designed and otherwise indefensible space in the HDB projects gives off no sense of risk.

Singapore is so powerful an alternative model for organizing urban society that it makes my head spin when I visit. I grow suspicious of both my attraction and my reservations. What the country has done is to place the strongest challenge to the generally accepted premise of European and North American liberal democracies, that a society based on ever-advancing individual rights and benefits will provide its citizens with the highest quality of life. Singapore stands that on its head. It is the individual's responsibility to work hard, to get an education, to stay healthy, to abstain from dangerous behavior, to look after the family, to own and maintain property; and all of this produces the best personal and collective outcomes. And a safe, smart city.

* * *

History is replete with gullible visitors returning from foreign lands claiming to have seen a future that works. Singapore, however, is not in the thrall of some charismatic dictator or corrupt strong man. For five decades it has been a functioning democracy, albeit with only one party in power all that time, the People's Action Party (PAP), founded by Lee Kuan Yew. After a decade's gap, his son, Lee Hsien Loong, became Prime Minister, and he remains in office. Elections are now increasingly contested. In 2011, the PAP received just 60 per cent of the vote. *The Economist's* Freedom Index grades the country three out of four, among the highest in Asia, which I find definitive. Whenever outsiders give them a hard time, Singaporeans nod to recent crackdowns on dissidents in their great rival, Hong Kong.

The sense one gets is that the next generation of Singaporeans will want to evolve towards a less directed society. There is an increasingly vigorous urban cultural scene and political life seems headed towards greater liberalization, although the primary political opposition tends to grumble about road tolls and how much or what kind of immigration to allow rather than challenging the basic socio-economic construct of the state. Singapore has grown rapidly by immigration. More than a third of the population is foreign-born. About 70 per cent of its citizens are Chinese, 17 per cent Malay, with a significant Tamil Hindu presence. A small and densely packed country, its early years were marred by interracial tension. About a fifth of the population consists of temporary workers and their status hangs as a long-term question for the country.

Lee Kuan Yew, in contrast to the nationalist spirits brewing elsewhere in Asia, was determinedly inclusive, knowing openness to be the only foundation for the modern society he wished to build. As a consequence, Singapore has boldly embraced multiculturalism. There are four official languages, which make subway station announcements a multilingual feast. Other than the preserved Chinatown and Little India downtown, Singapore has been keen to avoid ethnic enclaves. In what must be a unique form of social engineering, the Chinese, Indian and Malay occupancy profiles of each HDB project are carefully managed to reflect as far as possible the overall ethnic mix of the country. Affirmative housing action in the extreme.

One feels the legacy of Lee Kuan Yew everywhere. Singapore is still his creation. Born in 1923, he came of age during the Japanese invasion of the Second World War, an epochal event for Southeast Asia. He was born into a trading family, educated at Cambridge and trained as a lawyer. He returned to Singapore as it was moving towards independence from British rule. He was the founder of its dominant political party and prime minister for its formative decades. In later years, he became a prolific writer, setting out his social and political philosophy, a unique blend of Confucianism, Middle Temple lawyer, benefactor and entrepreneur. Interestingly, he derives from the same ethnic background as Deng Xiaoping, who sorted through the chaos of the post-Mao cultural revolution in China to lay the foundations of the economic juggernaut his country has since become. Both are Hakka Han, a distinct Chinese people originating mostly in southern China in the area around Guangdong. The two had a close relationship, with tiny Singapore acting as something of a mentor for mighty modern China.

Singapore first made its money as a port but soon added heavy engineering, shipbuilding, and other manufacturing activities. It still constructs about half the world's deep-sea oil platforms and it is the world's third largest oil refiner. Like all successful modern cities, it is having to negotiate the transition from making things to making ideas. Unlike most, it has a clear plan for doing so. Its top university, the National University of Singapore, stands high in the global rankings. Singapore trolls the world for talent, using as bait aggressive scholarships and incentives. It sends out its own elite to be exposed to the best in the world. On the edge of the university campus is One North, a highly successful, ever-expanding commercial science complex. The first cluster housed Biopolis, a dramatic complex designed by Zaha Hadid, to which the world's pharmaceutical companies and expertise were aggressively drawn with generous corporate and personal tax breaks. Opened a decade ago, Biopolis was followed by Fusionopolis, specializing in advanced engineering and materials science, and both are to be followed by Mediaopolis, a media/IT/digital cluster. There are also rumors of Nanopolis, devoted to nanotechnology and micro-engineering. One North is breathtaking. Every city in which we work seeks this forward-looking marriage of commerce and investment acumen with intellectual and scientific knowledge. Here it is, beautifully designed, spread over 200 hectares in a tropical forest.

Our firm's entrée to Singapore was winning an international competition for the master planning of a huge new urban waterfront district on the site of the container port south of downtown. In a characteristically bold move, the government had decided it was time to move the world's third-largest port to a more efficient location and create room for the city center to grow. Most world cities have barely figured out what to do with their pre-container port lands. The port area was vast. Frankly, we were skeptics, coming from timid Toronto, about the feasibility of the project. These were dismissed on contact with the briskly effective senior civil servant, Dr. Cheong Koon Hean, who appears to be responsible for everything urban in Singapore. "Congratulations on winning the competition," she said. "Now I have to give you Singapore 101. It's very simple. We have no oil, no gas, no resources, no agriculture and precious little water. All we have is brains." She smiled and sent us on our way. Of course, the same is true for every world city, though remarkably few recognize it.

When Sir Stamford Raffles took Singapore for the British 200 years ago, he found the Singapore River, a muddy tidal inlet filled with traders and fishers from across the region. He understood that inlet's global strategic advantage, sitting as it did at the juncture of the world's great trading routes. Rapid development followed. Raffles, like many a British colonialist, was a resolute urban improver. He commissioned a new city plan with disciplined streets, districts, public squares and botanical gardens, all characteristic of imperial attempts to bring order to an unruly world. Fine colonial buildings, now the government and cultural centers of the new Singapore, sprang up on the bluffs on either side of the river, including the famous Raffles Hotel, birthplace of the equally famous cocktail, the Singapore Sling. The inlet itself became a dense mass of sampans, floating businesses and homes. It was lined with warehouses—*godowns*—behind which were the *hutongs*, dense networks of narrow streets where locals lived and did business. Raffles insisted on five-foot covered sidewalks set into the fronts of these shops, chop houses, temples and bazaars to provide protection from the tropical heat and the regular tropical monsoon. The organized chaos along the inlet endured into the 1980s, by which time its food and wholesaling activities were declining with the changing business, demographic and retail structure of the city.

The decision to dam the Singapore River and replace its tidal, brackish water with a huge fresh-water reservoir is illustrative of Singapore's bold use of urban brainpower. The Marina Bay project was driven both by the imperative to sort out the sampan situation but also to lessen the country's strategically vulnerable dependence on fresh water supplied by Malaysia. From these objectives grew one of the largest, most ambitious waterfront developments anywhere.

Marina Bay expressed the country's desire to position itself as a world tourism and cultural destination. It was sparked in part by what Hong Kong was doing with major sites along its harbor. The Singapore-Hong Kong rivalry is one of those great inter-city stand-offs like London-Paris, New York-Los Angeles, Sydney-Melbourne, Toronto-Montreal. Each has its own mix of envy and disdain, caricature and truth. Singapore and its rival regularly exchange places in the rankings as to which, after New York and London, is the world's most significant financial center, as to which has the most dynamic business class, as to which is the more attractive place to live. They are currently competing to see which will become Asia's most dynamic cultural and entertainment hub. Hong Kong probably has the edge right now. It is moving ahead with an ambitious new cultural complex on its West Kowloon waterfront. So Singapore is playing catchup, looking to shed its straight-laced image. Marina Bay, with its urban lagoon, magnificent parks and striking cultural buildings, is its response.

On the city side of the bay, the sampans have been removed and the traders relocated into the incredibly cheap street-food hawker markets that dot the central city, places where I love to eat, even if I don't have a clue what I am eating. Sugarcane drink, yam paste ginko nut, Chinese porridge, peanut soup, popiah cockle. The *godowns* on either side of the inlet have been converted to tourist entertainment and eating destinations, some with real urban interest, some a bit hokey.

On the east side of the bay, an extensive new landfill was created, and it is now home to some breathtaking urban development projects. The dominant feature is the Marina Bay Sands Hotel and

Casino, designed by Canadian architect Moshe Safde. It is an exuberant complex of three curving hotel towers joined at the top by a long surfboard-shaped infinity pool. At the base of the complex is a vast retail center built to indulge the unbridled, incomprehensible Asian obsession with name brands, along with the entrancing, lily-shaped ArtScience Museum and a huge casino. There is nothing quite like it in the world.

Gambling was not something on which Lee Kuan Yew's view of responsible human behavior looked kindly. It was banned for many years until the realization that, particularly in Asia, tourism and gaming are strongly linked. Casinos are notoriously problematic urban buildings, so Singapore did not simply open the door and let it happen. The government structured the competition for the casino rights to ensure a spectacular design, and they certainly achieved that. They prohibited any casino building advertisement—I think unique in the world—so there are no garish, neon naming signs. There is actually nothing that advertises the casino's presence in the city, and while locals are not banned from using the casino they are charged a $100 tax per visit and strictly monitored for problem behavior. It is estimated that the casinos have added 1 per cent to national GDP. They have certainly transformed Singapore's tourism business. Yet again, the city has done something original and difficult, achieving positive results from the construction of a large-scale, centrally located casino, an outcome that has eluded every other major city.

To the east of the casino/hotel complex is Gardens by the Bay, the most dramatic large urban park created by any city in modern times, and perhaps the best example of how to turn a major urban open space into a destination with global appeal. Its 100 hectares of dense tropical landscaping represent plants and themes from each of Singapore's distinctive communities. It does not stop there. The planners added scale and imagination and a quirky landscape humor. Braided-metal, vine-draped super-palms spring up to house restaurants, along with innovative energy and hydroponic systems. Everything is linked together by treetop walkways. A pair of large, rolling, wave-like glass conservatories house imaginative presentations of local and global landscapes. Outside, the paths are lined with stalactites and stalagmites, tree barks and boles, all skillfully arranged to bring out anthropomorphic suggestions, helped along by subtle, and sometimes unsubtle, carvings of faces, animals and images. Nature is enhanced, improved and gently teased, harkening back to the follies and grottos characteristic of nineteenth-century landscape traditions that are now sadly forgotten or, worse, disdained in Europe and North America. It is hugely popular with both locals and tourists.

Gardens by the Bay reflects the interests of both of the city's founders. Stamford Raffles, the stereotypical British imperialist, was a dedicated botanist and zoologist and later a founder of the London Zoological Society. He loved the tropical paradise he founded by the bay. Lee Kuan Yew was said never to be happier than when adding to his garden city.

* * *

Singapore conducted none of the tangles of environmental assessments and other processes that bedevil huge urban projects in most cities. When we worked on the first plan for the Toronto waterfront, over 350 separate environmental assessments were identified as necessary, some provincial and some federal, creating a nightmare of needless complexity. Through relentless lobbying that number was reduced to about 200. The real enemy of city building is never some individual politician, landowner or site problem; it is the blob, the congealed mess of outdated and overlapping jurisdiction, the diffuseness of responsibility, the fact that simultaneously no one and everyone is in charge.

Singapore has no blob. The government decided to search out and apply the world's best environmental practices. Environmental assessments, in Singapore's view, are a way of avoiding the need to take responsibility for a needed initiative. There were no public meetings. Voting is mandatory in Singapore, so politicians are expected to know what the electorate thinks about issues and to convey public opinion to government. That is their democratic job, a role they see as more legitimate than that of responding to the concerns of the vocal and unrepresentative few who turn up at public meetings. Care is taken to ensure that the electorate is properly informed. The offices of the planning agency are spread across the city, each containing elaborate large-scale city models and information packages, with staff on hand to respond to questions.

The inlet was dammed ten years ago and now development around the huge lake at the center of the bay is firmly underway, accommodating the rapid expansion of Singapore's financial core. It is far from perfect. The fat, dark, heavy financial center emerging on the south shore is in need of a contemporary, Raffles-style design code, or some of the imagination of the Marina Bay Sands. The streets in this new district are too wide and in need of radical de-engineering, relics of old-fashioned traffic planning, empty and starved of traffic by the effectiveness of the war on the car. Jane Jacobs is nowhere to be seen in this district. Robert Moses, regrettably, would approve.

The Singaporeans I met are impeccably polite and well mannered, though exhibiting caution with outsiders. It takes an extended acquaintance before they will admit to anxieties, even if theirs are shared by any globally competitive city. Will we get lost in the competition, or forced out by the out-of-control cost of living? Can we welcome immigration but not get swamped by it? How can we limit the corrosive impact of the feckless, global hyper-rich, increasingly drawn to Singapore by its stability and low taxes? How can the city remain affordable for locals? And what about our distinct identity—is it civic or ethnic? Where is our past to be found in a city exploding with development? Can Lee Kuan Yew's inspiration take us all the way through the twenty-first century? Worryingly, the ruling family is for the first time engaging in tawdry public disputes. The modern world is moving in.

Intelligent Singaporeans have not attached their identity to a nostalgic, backwards-looking culture. Quite the contrary. "What next?" is their standard question. Asking it often leads them very quickly into territorial issues. They are running out of room and Malaysia sits less than a kilometer away. A high-speed rail line is planned to Kuala Lumpur and then on to the great cities of China, which could be a game changer, connecting Singapore to a large, less expensive labor pool and an abundance of land. Already the spread effect can be seen, with new development sprouting all over Malaysia's south shore. We recently helped one of Singapore's leading developers plan a large mixed-use community on the other side of the connecting causeway, a place destined to gain new centrality so close to the terminus of the high-speed rail line. Whether Malaysia will be content as Singapore's New Jersey is, of course, another matter. Relations are sometimes fraught.

Singapore keeps you at the top of your game. Its energy and competence can be exhausting; in our first visits, we found it difficult to relax and let go. Then some friends introduced us to the Singaporean mountains. Well, not really mountains, more like a ridge that gets perhaps a couple of hundred feet above sea level, with a wonderful ten-kilometer walk through a tropical forest full of flowering shrubs and colorful birds, and monkeys that go for your baseball cap. Along the way are beautiful, curved wood bridges over deep valleys and another section that takes you right up into the tree tops. The views over the island and the strait are entrancing. The succession of monuments and art is enticing. It is a good walk. The air feels fresh and mountainy, and at the end of the day the sun sets quickly. Singapore is one-degree north of the equator and its brightness gives way suddenly to a steamy, glowing evening light.

Our big break in Singapore, one that gave our firm its wider opening into Asia, came because the government's man in charge of the master plan competition for the southern waterfront redevelopment had gone to planning school at the University of Waterloo, just west of Toronto. When he was thinking about who in the world to invite to compete, he checked out Canadian firms and found us. We were one of twenty invited to participate in the first round, one of eight to make the second round, and one of two selected for the final face-off. Our little Toronto firm of seventy people was up against the mighty global office of one of the British architectural aristocrats, Foster and Associates, with over 5,000 employees. It is not every day you beat a lord at his own game, so to celebrate victory we headed out to No Sign Board, on Geylang Road.

Singapore has a reputation, somewhat deserved, for being a bit straight-laced. After all, it banned chewing gum. Lee Kuan Yew hated the slovenliness of gum chewing and the resultant black rings on the sidewalk. So do I, and generally I find his firm standards of urban behavior admirable. Every city, however, requires a few places where you can let your guard down, and we were delighted to find this sea-food place in the only slightly sketchy part of town of which I am aware. When taxi drivers take you there, they assume you are looking for something other than food. The story goes that it is called No Sign Board because it rose rather spontaneously out of an old gas station and car repair plant on a neighborhood main street. It never got around to having a name or a sign outside. It still doesn't. People just know.

Afterthought or not, the food at No Sign Board got better and better and more and more people showed up. Now there is a huge clear plastic tarp over the tables on the asphalt forecourt where the gas pumps used to be. The fish tanks are in the old car pits. The restaurant serves every crustacean in the ocean, along with its specialty, Pepper Crab. White pepper, not black. Such a fire in the mouth it has to be washed down by supersized beer bottles, 633 milliliters. What kind of insane precision is that, you ask on the third bottle. The air is hot and thick with humidity. The temperature in Singapore varies between thirty-one and thirty-two degrees Celcius, year-round. Big black Mercedes full of money pull into the lot. Everyone seems to know who is who. Now that the restaurant is a success, several anodyne branches have opened in the city center. Each has a signboard saying No Sign Board. Fine. But if you are in Singapore and need the perfect break from the island's disciplined perfection, head up to Geylang Road to the original.

We decide that No Sign Board is the ideal place to discuss Singapore's contribution to our perfect city. Big picture first. Singapore is a walking, talking political science course, prompting continuous debate among me and my colleagues and our clients about the greatest good for the greatest number, means and ends, competing concepts of liberty, top down and bottom up, cultural stereotypes and root causes. Also about the importance of leaders, because without Lee Kuan Yew it is hard to believe this remarkable place would have been created. Many new Asian cities have bold ambitions. Few achieve them. That is his legacy.

Angela Merkel, the German chancellor, recently observed that Europe has 7 per cent of the world's population, 25 per cent of its GDP, and 50 per cent of its social expenditures. All that and a rapidly aging population. We in Canada are not quite at that same pass, but there is a sinking realization in Europe that the continent can no longer afford the state it wants. If there is one fate Singapore is focused on avoiding, it is this trap of high entitlement expectations and dwindling tax generation. Indeed, some commentators have argued that what Lee Kuan Yew invented was the first genuinely original idea in practical political economy since the formulation of the post-war social democratic state. At the same time, Singaporeans seem to be solving another problem, one that any modern city dweller knows only too well: the problem of getting things done. Singapore, along with Seoul, Bangalore, Shanghai and Hong Kong, have far less difficulty than do cities in Europe and North America installing the essential equipment of the modern metropolis, in re-inventing its machine. They have radically tamed the presence of the private car. They are building the subways, airports, cultural buildings and parks that are contemporary versions of the great infrastructure legacies left to most of the world's European and North American cities by the Victorians and, later, the post-war builders. Too many of those cities have since lost either their capability or their nerve or, worse, they have created counter-narratives that disparage such world-class ambition.

A modern version of Robert Moses clearly rules in Singapore. Its consequences are largely admirable and its mistakes are readily correctable by a judicious application of Jane Jacobs. One thing is clear: it only works that way around. Moses first, Jacobs second. Are the mature liberal democracies of Europe and North America going to shift to top-down urban management? Unlikely. But, increasingly, as we will see, the successful cities of Western Europe and North America are evolving or experimenting with comparable forms of soft dictatorship in their city governments. It is easier in Singapore, no question, with their forcefully modernized machine, determinedly organized home and carefully constructed delight. A small, self-contained city-state can cultivate what locals characterize as a state-of-siege mentality to overcome any problem, domestic or foreign. "A tiny island with no friends," is how Singaporeans describe themselves in unguarded moments. I doubt that is true, but it is a useful story to have, using their "state-of-siege" mentality to get things done—in direct contrast to the West.

The inability of European and North American cities to manage their urban machinery, to create the physical, economic and intellectual infrastructures necessary to their lives, is steadily diminishing their ability to compete and to foster the social and economic dynamism without which problems of poverty, inequality and exclusion cannot be resolved. To say nothing of the top-down behavioral changes necessary to combat climate change. Very few of the things I admire in Singapore could be done in Europe or North America. We should not kid ourselves that this is not a problem. If you want to know to where the European and North American middle class has disappeared, it is to Singapore and its colleague cities. Not literally, of course, but this is where the energetic, productive, family-centric middle class of the future has found its home. The great and important debate about income inequality in big cities has missed the point that while inequality may be increasing in our cities, it is reducing dramatically when measured around the globe.

For my generation, questions about how to build a great city were often best answered by the Scandinavian countries. Lee Kuan Yew's creation, in the contemporary era, may be the Sweden of the tropics. But enough about Singapore. We get up from the table. After several beers, it is too easy for the little island city-state to magick you. It is a unique place, and its uniqueness cannot be directly transferred to another land. What can be copied are its energy, innovation and hard-headed understanding of how the modern city works. Let us get back to the European and North American part of our tour and see how, if at all, Western cities are meeting the challenges Singapore has posed. We turn to a city that has remade itself century after century, that stands second only to New York among global capitals, yet is perilously close to slipping in the rankings: London.

5

LONDON –
TURNING A CITY
AROUND

After New York's 5 train, what is the world's next most informative transit line? It has to be London's District Line, and we are heading east. The District Line is a barometer of London's socio-economic health. Starting in the leafy Thames-side urban villages of Richmond, Wimbledon and Kew, home to quiet, secure money, moving east it picks up the aspiring inner suburbs of Hammersmith, Putney and Fulham before diving below ground through the expensive squares and crescents of South Kensington. Twinned with the Circle Line through Westminster and the city it comes into its own again east of the Tower of London, falling off a precipitous cliff of wealth into east London, in which every successive underground station serves a measurably lower-income population, with shorter life expectancy and a higher percentage of immigrants. Pretty soon I am the rare aging white guy in the carriage, certainly the only one in a suit. When the train emerges back above ground the view out the window has changed completely. We trundle past flat, treeless housing estates with squat tower blocks, broken industrial parks, power lines and chimneys, roundabouts and traffic signals. This charmless mess is the landscape of east London. The mood sinks. And we are going way out east to Barking.

You have to love a place called Barking. Its official name is the London Borough of Barking and Dagenham. I have been asked to serve as a growth commissioner for the borough, which sounds very grand but really involves my getting an education about a city I thought I knew well. If you have not been to Barking, and I doubt one in a hundred-thousand visitors to London has, then go. You will learn something fresh about the city, as I did.

It is impossible not to smile when you get off the District Line. For starters, it is a relief to be away from central London: beneath the legacy architecture, what a dull, monotonous place it has become, a high-end consumption bazaar for tourists and rootless cosmopolitans. "Scrubbed clean by wealth," in the words of one of my partners. In Barking, you are immediately thrown into a real world of incredible energy and variety. The high street has been taken over by a vibrant street market run by traders from all over the world, most of them large, confident women with easy laughs. Is there a lot more public cheerfulness here than in the Bronx? It is the same global precariat but they look to be having a much better time, throwing gossip and jokes over their heads. The national origins of the people are evident in the window of the travel agent, who has posted exchange rates for Ghana, Nigeria, Poland, India, Bangladesh, Jamaica and Romania. You can buy anything on the street—food, clothing, appliances, trinkets—and it is inexpensive. Two dresses for £9. You can barely buy a coffee for that in the West End.

Barking has a long and storied history, starting as London's medieval fishing port and the site of a huge, now ruined monastery. Its independent existence came to an end with the steady eastward growth of the metropolis. Its twentieth-century character was determined by proximity to the docks, by the construction in the 1930s of the largest Ford car plant in Europe, and, of course, by its location on the east side, the wrong side, the backside of the smog-generating metropolis, a location that also entitled it to be the recipient of vast numbers of German bombs during World War II. It has remained one of the poorest districts in London, with over 40 per cent of its residents not making the London Living Wage, the index of what is required to live in the big city. The Ford plant drew its initial workforce from all over the United Kingdom, particularly from the north and from Ireland, giving the borough a distinct character, almost a place apart. That character was especially evident in the huge public housing complex, the Becontree Estate, which was built to provide those workers with 26,000 new homes, making it probably then the largest public housing estate in the world. Despite catastrophic job losses in both the Ford plant and the docks, the estate retains much of its original character, reflecting the social-democratic optimism of its birth. In its pleasant, curved streets sit homes with front and back gardens, built for working-class heroes, along with parks and shopping parades. The original Estate Tenant's Handbook is replete with instructions on the residents' responsibilities, with not a word on their rights, a document that would translate very readily to contemporary Singapore. For example,

4. The tenant shall keep the front garden of the premises in neat and cultivated condition. . .

8. The tenant shall clean the windows of the premises at least once every week.

As one observer has noted, "We shouldn't sugar-coat the paternalism here. There was a clear intention to encourage respectable living—pubs were restricted, and the virtuous domesticity of gardening heavily promoted. But remember, this was not, on the whole, a respectability which sat uneasily with the aspirations and characteristics of the vast majority of Becontree's new inhabitants." Something of that quality remains, even though many of the front gardens have been paved over for parking spaces.

Becontree's self-confidence largely evaporated in the 1970s with the collapse of the traditional U.K. economy. The necessary but agonizing restructuring advanced by Margaret Thatcher left places like Barking without jobs or pride, and the very success of Becontree in retaining its largely native English population contributed to the borough's reputation as a holdout of the traditional white working class. Nasty politics replaced that sense of cohesion in the community and the anti-immigrant British National Party (BNP) could for several decades rely on Barking and Dagenham as perhaps its strongest redoubt in the U.K. That nationalist strain persists. Barking was one of only five of London's thirty-three boroughs to vote for Brexit. Becontree remains determinedly white, even as the rest of the borough has become one of the most multicultural places on the planet. Which gives Barking that sense of fun and will make it a success again.

There are two town halls in the town center, one a fine example of Victorian municipal gothic, and the other of a 1930's *moderne* county hall design. Both buildings were built by people who knew what they were doing. Despite the borough's decline in the late twentieth century, they are now occupied by people who also seem to know what they are doing. You can tell the moment you walk into any municipal building in any city in the world whether the project for which you are retained stands a chance of success. The well-restored interiors of the town halls and the evident capability of the team assembled by the Labour Party council leader, the irrepressibly ebullient Darren Rodwell, give reasons for optimism. Rodwell, a man with an east end accent that should be bought by a museum, has determinedly fought back the racist/nationalist forces to fashion a real future for the borough.

The old and new town halls form the north and east faces of a new, well-designed town square. The south side is occupied by the Barking Central Library. As you may have noticed, I am a big fan of libraries. Properly equipped and managed, they are key building blocks in any smart city's economic development and immigrant settlement strategies, providing a hub for formal and informal skills training, for fostering community cohesion, and providing universal, free digital access. The U.K., even sophisticated London, seems however without an understanding of what to do with libraries in a modern urban culture. Almost a tenth of its municipal libraries have been closed in the past five years and their collective budgets have been reduced by 20 per cent. Barking, unfortunately, is no exception. From the exterior, the Central Library looks great, a modern, clean, welcoming building, with attractive-looking flats above. Inside, the heart sinks. Few shelves, fewer books, no computer screens, just piles of video cassettes, as if anyone uses them anymore, and a cheerless kid's play area. Half the space seems empty. A welcome contrast is DigiLab in the back of the library. It is a cramped, walk-in space, a hive of activity packed with all kinds of screens and digital gear all arranged around a lab table. DigiLab is run by Seun Oshinaike, one of those people who you know on first meeting is going to create the new Barking, the new London. He is tall, lean, handsome, late twenties, I would guess, with enormous energy. I ask him what he is doing in DigiLab: "Is it a teaching center, a skills development place? Or what?"

"No, no. You got it all wrong," he laughs. "It's a place for solving problems. And the biggest problem is, how are all the kids who are arriving in Barking from all over the world ever going to get a job?"

Seun traces his origins to Nigeria. He came to Barking as a teenager to finish high school, attended university but dropped out to start his own online digital businesses. He created Silent Secret, a clever app, an anonymous helpline that links troubled teenagers to supportive agencies. After a year, it had two million engagements in ninety countries and close to 60,000 active users. He has other apps in development, which he describes with great hand waves. His enthusiasm, however, is clearly in DigiLab. He has created after-school coding classes to teach local kids to do what he does. In a few months, he had 200 of them paying to attend regularly. One of his goals is to be among the top places in the borough that local companies approach to find digital talent, another is to supply at least 500 young people with the skills those companies want, and yet another is to duplicate his operation in other libraries and in other boroughs. Of course, he also wants to make money, "loadsa money," as they say in Barking, and have his coding-class students make money, too.

Much of the gear in the space, including the mini-robots that crawl over the table like electronic cockroaches, is designed to enable students to create computer games in real time. Seun believes that if he can capture their energy and imagination digitally—these kids are, after all, the actual consumers of such games—and translate it into a saleable product, DigiLab can become a business center in its own right. Being of a particular generation, I have little idea what he is talking about. But I do know how he is talking. Perfect.

The recognition that human capital is what makes a city great has not come easily to the United Kingdom, where a fractured, often ideologically driven education system had produced successively worse outcomes since the Second World War. About a decade ago, London decided it must do what it could to fix the quality of its public education system, establishing a program called *London Challenge* to transform the numeracy and literacy skills of its young population. The results are remarkable, with increases in measured student performance of more than 25 per cent. What is more impressive is that these improvements have taken place right across London, in rich and poor boroughs, right across the ethnic spectrum, with all groups showing dramatic improvements, from Chinese to African, native white to Bangladeshi, although native white students consistently underperform the rest. Barking's educational transformation has seen increases of up to a third in test outcomes spread evenly across its diverse ethnic groups. London's reversal of decline in its education system is quite unprecedented and cities like New York have noticed and are desperately trying to follow suit. What is fascinating is that despite extensive research on the process of this transformation, there is no agreement as to its causes. As a recent LSE report said simply, "something powerful, and slightly mysterious, has happened in London's schools." Was it increased math and English requirements and testing in primary schools, or partial privatization of educational delivery, or improved remuneration and training of teachers, or changes in classroom behavior, or better communication with parents, or new and renovated school buildings? Perhaps some combination of all of the above?

I find it interesting that similar initiatives have not resulted in comparable improvements in the great U.K. cities outside of London, including Manchester, Liverpool and Newcastle. In Scotland and Wales, literacy and numeracy standards remain in an abysmal slide. That suggests there could be a key and underappreciated ingredient at work in London: metropolitan-ness, combined with new immigrant aspirations. Barking is the most diverse borough in the U.K., with the highest number of new immigrants. London has been one of the world's fastest-growing mature cities, sucking in people from across the globe. People who live in big cities, who leave their native lands or their provincial homes for the metropolis, are motivated to succeed, are infected by aspiration. That is why their kids, if given the right opportunity, will do well. It is the reason why Toronto's public school students, educated in the most diverse large city in the world, test second only to Asian jurisdictions in the annual PISA math rankings. It is not the curriculum or the teachers or the school buildings or the money spent. Well, it is, but mostly it is the students and their parents, and the relative strength of immigrant families—a strength that protects against what is still the most deleterious precondition for academic achievement—the jobless single-parent family.

* * *

My work in London started in the late 1980s with Olympia and York, who had moved on from New York to its second great international project, Canary Wharf. You can now see the towers of Canary Wharf from the District Line, indeed, from almost anywhere else in London. Its distinctive cluster of high buildings is now replicated throughout east London as groups of high-rises and tower cranes surround each successive eastward transit station. I had a minor role in Canary Wharf, just as well because when the Reichmanns eventually went under with billions in debt, they only owed us £450, but I learned more there about the fundamental dynamics of cities than on any other project.

London, perhaps unique among major world cities, has turned itself around. For the greater part of its history, certainly its modern history, the dynamic of London's growth had been from the core of the old city to the west. More prosperous towns, better transport, better air quality, better air transport and the closer proximity of the larger part of the country had pulled the city west. Historically, it started with the squares and crescents of Mayfair, Regent Park, Marylebone, then moved onto Belgravia, Kensington, Chelsea, Notting Hill and out through those leafy District Line inner and outer suburbs, all the way to the affluent exurbs of Surrey. The east, to the extent that it was developed, was urbanized to a remarkable degree by public housing. Boroughs like Barking and its neighbors, Newham and Tower Hamlets, had up to 90 per cent of their housing stock in council (public) ownership, and by the 1970s that statist housing management had calcified urban class and income divides, with tragic consequences once the traditional employment supports for the working class faded away.

As in New York, the retreat of London's traditional shipping and manufacturing activities left a vast stock of unused land at the center of the city, especially in the docklands. All over the world, great harbor-side sites were rendered redundant by the invention of the shipping container, the one technological innovation that has had a more profound effect on the structure of the modern city than any other. Container cranes and storage, and the much larger ships that carry them, no longer fit in the old urban ports. The London docks were abandoned, over the course of about ten years, leaving twenty-two square kilometers of vacant land along the Thames. Schemes abounded for the repurposing of this space. The left had visions of yet more council estates, the right wanted get-rich-quick developments, and the urbanists proposed fussy little townscapes. Predictably, nothing happened. Local councils were ill-equipped to deal with a problem requiring large-scale solutions. As a result, Margaret Thatcher placed all the land in an unelected development agency reporting directly to her government and gave that agency a remarkably free hand and plenty of tax concessions. She abolished the Greater London Council completely, and the local councils effectively, because they got in her way. It was what she liked to call "the smack of firm government," a smack that divides opinion to this day. But it was remarkably effective.

Canary Wharf was from the first an absurd venture. When the Reichmanns and their team announced their plans to build a new financial center with millions of square feet of office space, enough to rival the City of London, on a derelict dock basin several miles east of the tower, skepticism abounded. The only road access was down the aptly named Narrow Street and the transit service was a quaint but inadequate Docklands Light Railway that did not really connect to anywhere those office workers might want to go. High-brow opinion was appalled that the Reichmanns wanted a forty-two-storey building that could be seen from everywhere. How crass, how foreign to the texture of the city, how American, despite it being called Canada Square. Yet the Reichmann's global perspective enabled them to understand more clearly than the locals what the machine of the city needed: big floor-plate office buildings to accommodate the trading style of the "big bang" deregulated financial services industry. One of the consequences of Thatcher's emasculation of the local and London councils was that there was no empowered planning authority left to review and approve the plans prepared by Reichmann's team. Happily, the Prime Minister and her able minister for local government, Michael Portillo, not only liked what they saw but relished the review role, making useful height, layout and design suggestions, perhaps the first time a Prime Minister had acted as chief planner. It is taking the rest of the country longer to understand how significant Canary Wharf has been to the future of their capital. Some probably never will. In right-minded U.K. architectural circles, it is still as vulgar to express an admiration for Canary Wharf as it is to harbor affection for the Royal Family.

Among the colleagues and, later, friends I worked with on the London Docklands, David Taylor stood out. Trained as an architect, he went on to be the first head of the U.K.'s urban regeneration agency and a successful developer and entrepreneur in his own right. He was the most effervescent and connected man I knew in England. At the time of the Tony Blair government, he had contacts right to the top as a chief advisor to Deputy Prime Minister John Prescott. He would call me when he knew I was in town. "Whatya doing this evening?" Usually, I was going to order room service and watch a football game on my hotel TV. He always had a better idea. He would take me for tea on the terrace of the Houses of Parliament, to the Directors Box at Preston North End football club, to one of Tony Wilson's lunatic new Manchester music happenings, to meet Tony Blair at some handshake event or Ken Livingston at the London Zoo. He loved shocking me with these casual invitations. And then one night it was, "Howdya like to come to the Palace and met the Prince?" It was not quite as easy as that. Passports had to be submitted, questions asked, but early that evening we pulled up to St. James Palace in David's stretch Jaguar.

Prince Charles, in his urbanist phase, had been a vocal critic of Canary Wharf. Indeed, it would have been hard to find any development more offensive to his notion of the perfect city. He dismissed it with a wave of the wrist in one of his TV documentaries. At St. James's Palace, he gave a little speech to the twenty of us in the room about urban villages, explaining his arts-and-crafts, whole-grain, carefully textured view of urban development. He did not make a lot of sense but then we could see he was nervous, always fussing with his cuffs and straightening his back. He stood on a dais below the famous Holbein portrait of Henry VIII, who stared down at us, bejeweled, hawk on shoulder, legs apart, hips pushed forward, red beard bristling, codpiece prominent. The very model of a king. The comparison was unavoidable.

It was the worst period of Charles' breakup from Diana. Toe-curling details of his intimate conversations with Camilla had been phone-hacked and splashed over the tabloid press the day before. So I do have to cut him some slack, though he did seem pathetic. And while I am at it, what a nightmare is St. James's Palace! All crenellated and Tudor from the outside, a dark, dank, scuffed and faded maze on the inside, with successive junk rooms of colonial appropriation. Endless walls hung with wheels of Matabele spears and roundels of Gurkha daggers, tribal headdresses and Hussars' banners, placed haphazardly between vast paintings of the Battle of Rourke's Drift. Like some imperialist's discount emporium. No sane person could last a minute in there, let alone Diana. The food, however, was fine. Doubtless from the Prince's organic gardens at Highgrove. I fondly remember the grilled fennel.

* * *

The success of Canary Wharf is not only that it added to the city's urban iconography, nailing down the east end of the great Thames view from Westminster Bridge, but that it became the fulcrum for the regeneration of east London. Canary Wharf's critical mass was the precondition for turning London's urban growth dynamic east-wards. It demonstrated the importance of understanding the city as a machine, of appreciating that only an intervention of enormous power and scale can redirect the momentum of a great metropolis. That new direction depended on a project large enough to require and partly pay for the eastward expansion of London's public transport system. The initial DLR transit service to Canary Wharf was rapidly overloaded by the demands of its thousands of new office workers. That dramatic increase in ridership led to an accelerated extension of the Jubilee Line, the underground route that would connect Canary Wharf to the heart of London, networking with other lines and with main-line train stations. So successful was Canary Wharf and the neighboring devel-opments it spawned that the Jubilee Line, too, is now packed. The continuing success of docklands redevelopment has led to the con-struction of Crossrail, probably the most ambitious transit investment in any city.

Crossrail is a 118-kilometer, high-speed subway extending east-west across the entire London city-region, essentially from west of Heathrow out to Barking and beyond. With limited stops and fast, frequent ser-vice, Crossrail, recently renamed the Elizabeth Line, will change the geography of the city, tying all of its principal destinations together and accommodating the growth of London by relieving the long-distance demands on the existing Underground. It will be followed by Crossrail 2, with a roughly NE/SW alignment. The Crossrail initiatives are extremely expensive, complex urban projects, the kinds of under-takings that often go wrong in advanced cities around the world.

There are a number of reasons why London, unlike many other cities, including Toronto, Sydney and even New York, can pull off projects of this magnitude. First, it has access to top-flight profes-sional and contracting teams. London is perhaps the world center of urban engineering and it has never stopped building its transit sys-tem, modernizing and extending its lines, a practice that has kept a body of expert labor employed and available. Transport for London, known as TfL, the city's transit development and management agency, is without a doubt the most capable agency of its kind in the Western world, with a competence that has engendered remarkable independence and innovation in transit planning, construction and operations. London also understands how to allocate the risks of major projects. It has sophisticated tendering and procurement techniques that properly assign design, cost, time and construction risks to the appropriate public or private sector partners, reducing the chance of the nightmare cost-overruns that customarily bedevil major projects. They are not afraid of privatization. They have learned how to use it smartly. And beneficiaries contribute to the costs. It was Canary Wharf's capital contributions to both the Jubilee Line and Crossrail that supported the business case for approval of government funding. Of course, London's applications for national funding are helped by its standing as the nation's capital, something that also benefits Paris, but not New York, Sydney, Toronto or Manchester.

All of these advantages notwithstanding, the critical ingredient of London's success is the confidence of its municipal government. Nothing in a city succeeds like success. The ability to pull off a complicated project is the supreme test of local government. London has done it time and again. It helps that, after the creative disruption of the Thatcher years, London has evolved the best governance structure of any major Western city, a two-tier system in which the upper tier, the city-wide Greater London Authority, is responsible for big things—major transport, economic development, housing policy and strategic planning. It oversees the larger metropolitan region, the full extent of the real city. The lower tier, consisting of thirty-three boroughs, is responsible for social service delivery, environmental management, and local planning matters. It is an eminently sensible division of civic labor. The structure of the Greater London Authority is made up of the elected mayor, twenty-five elected members of the London Assembly and roughly the same number of appointed members. The mayor has the political and administrative latitude to execute his or her agenda through nine hand-picked deputy mayors, people with impressive real-world track records and political savvy. There are checks and balances but the mayor is clearly entrusted with the necessary powers and authority. The current Deputy Mayor for Housing, James Murray, is only thirty-one years old, whip-smart and full of energy. That's how big cities get built.

When I chatted with then-mayor Ken Livingstone at the London Zoo he had just introduced the congestion charge. London was among the first cities to take the bold move of making drivers pay for urban road use. The congestion-charge system was operated by private contractors and it employed what was then novel plate-recognition technology. It had been an election promise, lightly considered and scarcely noticed. Livingstone had absolutely no idea what the public reaction would be, whether or not it would work, whether or not he had committed political suicide. It was either a foolhardy or a courageous political act. It has turned out to be the latter, a lesson to the urban world in the importance of empowered mayors. The machine of a big city can only be directed in a political framework that allows for big decisions.

London extended its capability for urban innovation throughout the mayoralties of Livingstone and Boris Johnson, bringing out the best in both of them before they later decayed in national political life. It is now being energetically extended under Mayor Sadiq Khan. The introduction of the Oyster Card, a quick and easy way to pay for transit, the provision of mobile phone service for commuters, the sharing of real-time information across the entire transit system, and the skillful privatization of service delivery are advances that first eluded and then were copied by most other cities. London has undertaken radical remakes of great public spaces such as Trafalgar Square and the London Eye. It has built fast arterial bike routes throughout the city. Coming soon is an inspired lighting plan for the bridges of the Thames. A city that can get in the habit of behaving this way is fortunate, channeling the get-it-done spirit of Robert Moses in service of a more sympathetic, contemporary urbanism.

I have been travelling to London for business almost ten times a year for three decades now. It has been fascinating to watch the city regain its confidence and resume its historic place at the summit of global cities. For long decades after World War II, London was thought to be finished. It was losing population until the mid-1980s, awash in social discord and economic pessimism.

The great urban planner and academic Sir Peter Hall wrote my favorite book for understanding greatness in cities. In *Cities in Civilisation,* he tracks the emergence of classical Athens, Shakespearean London, turn-of-the-century Berlin, Hollywood, Silicon Valley, and many others in an effort to identify the specific causes of their rise. In each case, he finds a significant surge in immigration coincident with the introduction of some new technical invention, business structure, or trade opportunity. He gives example after example. London's seventeenth-century prominence is owed to the arrival of Dutch merchants, the invention of the joint stock company, and new sailing techniques. Hollywood blossomed from the diaspora of Europe's Jewish culturati, the invention of new moving picture technology, and a sunny climate. These combinations establish the "innovative milieu" that inspires transformational urban change. In London of the 1990s, it was a massive deregulation of financial services, an influx of American financial know-how, along with borough-filling immigration.

Sir Peter Hall, a vital, charming man of unbounded curiosity, was an effective doer as well as a thinker, rare among planning academics. He was one of the first to understand that the scale of the 1980s Docklands problem required large-scale government intervention. He was one of the creators of the highly autonomous, financially innovative urban regeneration agencies formed to make projects like Canary Wharf happen. He understood the dynamics of the urban machine, how important big projects are to driving urban change. He foresaw that without a substantial Canary Wharf development there would be no Jubilee Line to east London. Without the Jubilee Line there would have been no appropriate site for the Olympics. And without the Olympics there would have been no transformation of one of the largest areas of contaminated, abandoned, centrally located urban land in Europe.

* * *

London won the bid for the 2012 Olympics in 2005. At the core of its bid was the plan to transform the Lea Valley, a leftover mess of junk industry, wrecking yards, polluted rivers and abandoned canals north of Canary Wharf. The Lea Valley had always been one of the most intractable barriers to the eastern spread of urban regeneration. Victorian London stopped on its western bank, with council house London starting to the east. Picking it as an Olympic site was a bold move. I had scoped the area for the Reichmanns in the 1990s and told them not to give it another thought. I can imagine the faces of members of the Olympic selection committee when they saw how unprepossessing a site London proposed to develop.

But the city understood that the Lea Valley's transformation was only going to happen with the scale and impetus of an Olympic preparation. Contemporary city builders tend to frown upon Olympics, with good reason. Rare is the city that can pull off the event within budget, without painful disruptions to local communities, and without being left with unexpected costs and underperforming revenues. London proved an exception. Its large athletic facilities—the stadium, velodrome and aquatic center—enabled an almost total clearance of the center of the valley. Most of those facilities have been retained and passed on to new users. The pedestrian circulation system necessary for Olympics has provided the sinews of a large, new London park. The Olympic Village beside the transport complex at Stratford has been transferred, after some missteps, to the private sector. Dense and monotonous, it is not the most attractive housing complex in the world but it stands as a working residential community in the midst of what had been industrial wilderness. Most interestingly, the Olympic communications center, a huge, million-square-foot shed, has been converted into a high-tech business incubator and academic center known as Here East. It is home to branches of several London and national universities and dozens of start-up companies, and it acts as the terminus of a vector of high-tech development that runs west through the Tech City cluster in Shoreditch to the new Google headquarters at Kings Cross.

The official name for this new urban district is Queen Elizabeth Park. It has also been called Olympicopolis, a name I rather like as it expresses the roots of this transformation. Alison Nimmo has said that

Queen Elizabeth Park is "true to the great tradition of London development" in that it is built "at the scale of historical estates." Nimmo should know. She was the person at the Olympic Development Agency most responsible for getting the site built and then refitting it for its current existence. She now has the best development job in the country, perhaps in the world, as Chief Executive of The Crown Estate, the monarchy's land holdings. The monarchy holds a lot of land.

I have dinner with Alison, a long-time colleague and friend, and her partner, Chris Brown, himself an innovative developer, at my favorite London restaurant, Caffe Caldesi, on Marylebone Lane. I often eat here by myself at the bar. Pasta del giorno and a rocket and parmesan salad, washed down with a glass of Nero d'Avola. With its pleasant, big-city buzz, you never feel alone at the restaurant when you eat on your own. This time, however, we eat upstairs, white-table-cloth fancy. Nimmo speaks of her "estate view" of great London development. The district in which we dine, Marylebone, has been the property of the estate of the descendants of Baron Howard de Walden, an admiral of Queen Elizabeth I, since the early eighteenth century. It remains in the family to this day. To the south is Mayfair, held since the seventeenth century by the descendants of the Duke of Westminster and still managed by the Grosvenor family. To the north is Regent's Park, a huge estate stretching down to the core of London, developed by the Prince Regent in the early 1800s as a means of paying off his gambling debts. Nimmo carries the keys for that estate, among many monarchical legacies.

In her view, both Canary Wharf, which is still under unified ownership, and Queen Elizabeth Park are manifestations of that established tradition of developing large parts of London under a single coordinated development regime and holding them for the long-term. "Though Canary Wharf is still a bit sterile, isn't it?" she says. It is a common critique of the development's corporatist feel. "Better than it was," I mumble. I am still defensive of Canary Wharf even though I had so minor a role in its creation. I go on to slag the arid, aristocratic, exclusionary feel of Belgravia, one of her great estates behind Buckingham Palace.

Nimmo is the most prominent woman in property development in the U.K. It has always been a man's game, with an established culture that includes drinking unfathomable amounts, political incorrectness, and an inclination not to football but to the rougher game of rugby. Nimmo not only made it in this world, but she is the only one of my acquaintances to make it to the walls of the National Portrait Gallery. How did she rise? It was not easy. I once heard Nimmo give a jaw-dropping speech on what it was like to be an early female arrival in the male-dominated real estate world. But time is changing the development industry, along with everything else. You cannot bully a building into being built anymore. While force and energy are still required, patience, persuasion, persistence, partnerships and participation are increasingly what it takes. Are those attributes more female than male?

It is a fine evening so I walk back to my hotel after dinner. I am struck again by the evidence of extreme wealth in London. One of the de Walden Estate's cleverest projects has been to upgrade the retail tenancies along both sides of Marylebone High Street, transforming what once was a meat-and-potatoes high street into an upscale shopping experience. It is essentially a luxury mall on a regular public street. The local grocers and merchants have been moved out in favor of specialty food stores, the bacon-and-egg cafés have given way to *recherché* coffee houses. Few national chain stores have been permitted; an exception is a discretely contained Waitrose supermarket. Marquee fashion houses and luxury shoe stores boast exquisitely designed shop windows featuring one or two exquisitely arranged objects. What was once a pleasant, comfortable neighborhood street now feels out of reach. I am reasonably well off and even I can't afford to shop here. I live in fear that Daunts, the best bookstore in the world, will be the next to be bounced from the street, leaving me without a reason to visit.

This is London's biggest problem. Like all big cities at the top of the spike, it attracts global wealth on such a scale that its property market is inflated beyond the means of the local population. Nowhere does the price exaggeration seem as extreme as London. Over the past twenty years, house prices have multiplied six times, and in the wealthier areas ten times. Huge sectors of the city are now beyond limits for regular human beings, including all of the West End, Marylebone, Kensington and Chelsea. Increasingly, the once middle-class districts are following suit. New development is almost exclusively for the super-rich. In London, as in New York, Paris, Sydney, Vancouver and elsewhere, property has become commodified. Its purpose has evolved from straightforward residential use to that of an asset class designed for storing wealth. A classic London square is like a piece of fine art, no longer for living with or looking at, but for the owning by Russian kleptocrats, Gulf princelings, Asian oligarchs and other assorted billionaire refugees.

More and more, Londoners are forced into the rental market. As a result, rents in London are already twice the national average and have climbed 19 per cent in the past five years. Half of London's tenants pay more than half of their disposable incomes in rent. This despite the lowest unemployment and worklessness rates in decades. Like his New York counterpart, Bill De Blasio, London's new mayor, Sadiq Khan, aided by Deputy Mayor James Murray, is pushing dramatic new housing development and affordability policies. He wants to crank the rate of housing production to 65,000 a year from its current level of 25,000, fast-tracking applications that include at least 35 per cent affordable housing and giving other developers a hard time. It's too early to tell for sure, but these policies seem to be turning the new housing market around.

Despite its housing costs, London's population continues to grow, by 13 per cent in the past decade. It still sucks in the best national and international talent. Twenty-two per cent of all U.K. graduates move to London. Manchester and Birmingham, major university towns, retain 3 per cent each. London is the destination of a third of all immigrants to the United Kingdom. That is another reason why its unaffordability is of such concern. London has been very successful in adding high-end employment, but that very success in attracting such additional house purchasing power just contributes to the problem.

The city dominates the national economy and essentially pays all the bills for it, contributing 26 per cent more in tax revenue to the national exchequer than it consumes. No other city or part of the country makes a net contribution. Financial services, one of London's key economic activities, alone contributes 12 per cent of the national corporate tax take. The whole of the U.K. thus has a stake in London's ability to accommodate still more high-end jobs and immigration.

Which leads us to the greatest question regarding the future of London and the U.K.—Brexit. It is probably too early to tell whether the country will lose its future in the same way that it gained an empire, "in a fit of absence of mind," but Brexit cannot be good news for London, threatening its core industry, restricting its supply of skilled labor and undermining its attraction to the world's young, success-minded immigrants. In a presage of the Trump election, all of the growing, younger, urban, future-oriented parts of the U.K. voted to remain in the European Union. The declining parts of the country, the very districts that are most dependent on EU funding, voted to leave, and their view prevailed. Those declining areas are now joined in a dis- like and resentment of London despite—or, perhaps, because of—the fact that it pays the bills. This does not bode well for a city that needs substantial national government funding for the big projects that keep it among the world's best.

National resentment, the hollowing-out effects of absentee wealth, the expense of its real estate, an aversion to more immigration and the comfort of its outdated mythologies combine to suggest that London, of all cities, is most likely to slip from its high ranking. It should not be counted out. London has an extraordinarily resilient history as the first recognizably modern city, an imperial capital, a global manufacturing and global financial center. But the new world, dominated by Asia, may not need it quite so much anymore, and may not be forgiving if the U.K. mishandles the next great turn of history's wheel.

I stop at Daunts to get a book for my trip up north. A quick scan of tables confirms its global bookstore primacy, never failing to provide me with something fascinating. I have an unexpected hour before heading to Euston Station, so I take a coffee and my sketchbook to a little park tucked behind the high street. A play area at one end and a formal flower garden at the other, all under a grove of tall, gnarled plane trees. It is an eighteenth-century park, once a burial ground with an ancient carved limestone mausoleum that remains beside the path, a secret garden in the heart of a city that has seen a lot of history. I try to capture the shading of the tomb, the angle of the plane branches. Not very well. Somewhere in that familiar space between not bad and not good enough. It does not matter. All is peace, delight at the center of a city I love.

6

MANCHESTER – ONCE UPON A BOMB

Manchester. An increasingly short train ride from London but a huge urban distance. The city where David Taylor, Alison Nimmo, Chris Brown and I got started in the United Kingdom. The city whose story begins with a bomb. There is nothing quite like a bomb for testing a city, a big bomb on a bright June mid-morning in 1996.

Manchester has always been a place bigger than it is, one of the reasons the Irish Republican Army chose it as the target for so large a bomb. It is arguably the world's first industrial city, rising to prominence in the nineteenth century much as Shanghai, Shenzhen and Singapore have in our time. It owes its ascent to technological innovation—the spinning jenny—an invention that delivered as much disruption as robotics and artificial intelligence promise to today. Manchester developed an enormous manufacturing base, aided by imperial markets and imperial preference. It was the meeting place of Marks and Spencer, of Rolls and Royce, of Engels and Marx. It was first among the great nineteenth-century British cities to challenge the country's land-owning aristocracy with commercial wealth. The splitting of the atom (Edward Rutherford) and the invention of the computer (Alan Turing) happened in Manchester, and just a few years ago it was home to the discovery of graphene, expected to be the magic material of the twenty-first century. Always a free-thinking intellectual, cultural and political center, it is the birthplace of free trade and the *Guardian* newspaper, and it has engaged in an endless rivalry with London, demanding to be heard in a country so dominated by its capital.

Manchester was hit hard by the industrial decline of the 1970s and 1980s. The economic restructuring of those decades gave it new fame for unemployment, for decaying *Coronation Street* neighborhoods and for a raucous, angry music scene. One of the few benefits of its decline was that its wonderful stock of older commercial buildings, particularly from the interwar period, went largely untouched, with no tide of post-1960s progress to wipe them away. Manchester's core retains the feel of the once-proud industrial cities of America—Pittsburgh, Cleveland, Detroit or Buffalo—except that the wrecking ball has been kinder.

The bomb could have redressed that balance. It was the biggest bomb ever seen in post-war Britain, a large truckload of fertilizer laced with jet fuel and primed with semtex. It was left by an IRA cell outside Marks & Spencer in the city center midday on a summer Saturday. The streets were packed with shoppers and tourists and global soccer fans headed for the next day's European Cup game between Germany and Russia.

The bombers phoned a coded warning message to local radio stations ninety minutes before detonation, a tactic designed to absolve them of responsibility for any resultant carnage. Fault would lie with inept security services, or so they hoped. Mercifully, the security was not inept. Police showed extraordinary competence by evacuating 75,000 people from the area in under half an hour without a hint of panic. The only casualty was the bomb-disabling robot that was approaching the truck as the bomb went off. There were many people with minor injuries. A boy lost a finger to a flying glass shard but it was subsequently re-attached. Disaster had been adverted. Almost.

Manchester's core was the prime casualty of the bomb. The central retail district was heavily damaged. The blast stretched over a one-kilometer radius and put more than 600 businesses out of commission. I developed a macabre fascination for the effects of the explosion, a fascination one could indulge without guilt, since, unlike most urban bombings, it had claimed no lives. High-rise buildings were split open down their spines like lobster. The differential pressure of the blast wave threw elevator doors out a few inches further on each successive floor. I scrambled up to the cafeteria on the top floor of the former M&S tower to find a terrible beauty of broken glass and wrecked furniture. The grand glass cupolas on top of the magnificent nineteenth-century Royal Exchange and Corn Exchange buildings were popped off like lids on coffee cups, landing a few feet off center. Apparently solid walls had been whipsawed a meter or more and stood precariously, ready to collapse. Streets were full of rubble and broken vehicles. Oddly, right next to Marks & Spencer, in which there was nothing left that was larger than your hand, was a small café with its hastily abandoned coffee and cakes still on the table.

By global standards, Manchester's devastation does not compare with today's Aleppo, Beirut, Mosul or Damascus, or with 9/11 New York. Nor does it compare even to my dim memories of holding my mother's hand through the post-war piles of rubble in what had been the center of Exeter. But a major city had nonetheless been knocked out cold and left with a very big hole at its heart. I had been up at a cottage in northern Ontario, sunlight breaking through the cedars, when I got a call from Howard Bernstein, then deputy chief executive of Manchester. "There's been a bomb. Can you get over?" I got on a plane.

Not that Manchester did not already know what to do. To overcome something as devastating as a bombing, a city needs three things: good people, a good plan and money, lots of it. It was clear that Manchester was well on its way towards all three by the time I got off the plane. The fact that no one had been killed meant that there was no necessity for a period of grieving and memorial, an experience in stark contrast to New York after 9/11 or Oklahoma City after the devastation of the Federal Building. Here, civic leaders could get right into rebuilding, and they had their act together.

To find the origin of Manchester's rebuilding strategy you have to go back to the early eighties, before the bomb. The north of England was prostrate from two decades of deindustrialization and rife with labor trouble as, one after another, the pillars of the industrial economy gave way. Docking, textiles, coal mining, heavy engineering, steelmaking—all that was solid melted into air. Most northern cities, notably Glasgow, Liverpool and Sheffield, had adopted a militant stance against the government of Margaret Thatcher, whom they saw as responsible for their industrial decline. Manchester, perhaps by virtue of being the world's first industrial city, and with its long traditions of independent political thought, uniquely understood that the past was not coming back and that the task was to lay the foundations for its re-emergence as the world's first post-industrial city.

The strategic plan prepared in the mid-eighties for the renewal of the city center was remarkable in the world of city planning for how much had been achieved even before the bomb. If it had not been so perilous, it might have been considered a fortuitous act of urban renewal. We often found ourselves wishing it had blasted away more, particularly of the Arndale Centre, a charmless 1960s shopping center at ground zero. Manchester's strategy involved building a new economy, one theme at a time. It started with the regeneration of Castlefield, the old canal district. Its old warehouses and proud Victorian engineering infrastructure was being converted into a hip eating and cultural neighborhood, creating an environment that would spur inner-city residential redevelopment. Bridgewater Hall was built as a new home for the Halle Orchestra. To promote tourism, the city radically improved its conference, meeting and hotel facilities, making Manchester the most attractive U.K. meeting venue outside of London. Next came sports, not just the famed Manchester City and United teams, but the clear positioning of the city as the sports capital of the country with leadership in cycling and the Paralympics. Servicing all of these initiatives was a bold new airport with a runway forced into a greenbelt over the objections of environmentalists. It secured the city's position as the leading alternative to Heathrow, and with it came a burst of new jobs. As in other world cities, the airport has become Manchester's second largest locus of employment after the city center.

Rebuilding the post-bomb city center, then, did not start from scratch. Manchester already knew what to do, and it was doing it. It also had the people to do it, a tribe of its own. Two failed pre-bomb bids for the Olympic Games and a successful bid for the Commonwealth Games were instrumental not only in delivering key infrastructure but, more importantly, in developing a Manchester team. To a far greater extent than most cities, Manchester has been able to get its key public, business and institutional leadership to take combined ownership of its future. Any great city has to be big and open enough to generate, retain and attract remarkable people. When the bomb went off, Manchester's political leadership pulled in the necessary energy and expertise from outside City Hall, people with whom they already had established relationships: Sir Alan Cockshaw, the straight-talking head of Amec, a major international engineering and construction company, and his then colleague David Taylor; Mike Oglesby, the principal of a large, locally based development company; Alison Nimmo, then at KPMG; and the fabled twenty-four-hour party person, Manchester-sound music producer and impresario, Tony Wilson. These people were doers, not shouters or critics. Their networks crossed political, cultural and business boundaries. They had played together before and won. They gave the city a voice and a momentum that government alone could not have managed.

* * *

Another of the projects on which the tribe had played together and won was a complete and hugely successful remake of Hulme, an inner-city district just south of Manchester's center that has gone through several incarnations even in my lifetime. Hulme had been a nineteenth-century slum district rotten enough to catch the notice of Engels in *The Condition of the English Working Class*. It had undergone a massive clearance in the 1960s. I remember driving through Hulme after the clearance but before new construction. Nothing remained in this huge flat area except for the grid of streets and the occasional massive red sandstone school building, neo-classical and intimidating. And on every corner, like the last tree in a clear-cut, the pub. No people, no houses, just the pubs. It was a landscape so surreal, so brutally cleansed that it became a staple location for English working-class movies of the times.

These empty spaces were filled in the early 1970s by a 200-acre modernist council housing estate. It had received all of the requisite architectural awards in its day. City councilors and their architects had gone to Bath to observe the perfect dimensions of its Regency crescents and brought them home to size up their new palaces for the poor. To see their plans for a working-class New Jerusalem was to realize how deeply they hated what had been there before, the tight streets and blocks and back alleys of a terrace-housing world; its smells, its culture, its cramped constraints. How improvable new residents would be if subjected to correct architecture. For those who might not immediately get the point, the developers named the new buildings The Nash, The Adam and so forth. Mile-long linked and nested crescents of housing, five-storeys high, with the front doors of every unit opening to a walkway that stretched the length of the crescent. They were streets in the sky, walkways accessible only by elevators at the ends of the crescents. The end of this new dawn was not long in coming. Cities do not take well to architectural theory. When the contractors had finished assembling the system-built housing, they left on the site a baffling array of uninstalled reinforcing rods, connector plates, and other hardware, like extra bits in a model airplane kit. Damp, rust and structural failure took over from there. The streets in the sky became security traps as the elevators endlessly broke down. They filled with trash and excreta. At its peak, some 15,000 people had lived in Hulme. When we got there in the late eighties it was down to less than 5,000, a population of students, squatters and turnouts from institutions. The council no longer seriously tried to collect rent. More than half the units had been abandoned. Many had burned out, leaving smoke scars on the face of the crescents. Itinerant travelers with battered vans and mangy horses moved into the spaces between the buildings of the estate.

Our firm had worked in a lot of bad and beaten places, but I was more unsettled in Hulme than in post-riots Detroit or 1970s Brooklyn. It had become renowned in the national press for drug crime and murder, with both suspects and victims lost in the inscrutable geography of the estate. The monumental, formal eeriness of its architecture provoked primal terror. When we walked around to take photographs, one of us would keep the car running.

Hulme was an extreme example of an urban god that failed. It would need to be cleared and built again less than two decades after it had been cleared and built with such high hopes. I was haunted by those hopes. The road to Hulme had been paved with good intentions. Behind the new architectural forms and the innovative building systems was an idealism, a thirst for social betterment entirely lacking in more utilitarian social housing developments. And yet it stood like the Berlin Wall, as a gruesome testament to the failures of the twentieth century. I found myself wondering if part of it should be preserved as a place of mandatory professional pilgrimage for architects, planners and social-housing estate advocates. A place for us all to learn humility and wonder what egregious errors subsequent generations will find in our work.

By the time we started on Hulme, it had been studied to death. We reviewed endless analyses of failed housing conditions and social policies. Our own detailed analysis of the neighborhood made it clear there was little or nothing to maintain. A large monoculture of poor, municipally managed social housing tenants is no community. It has no depth and no resilience to the forces of physical decay and social decline. The crescents and the system-built housing were impossible to repair. All that could be kept were the legacies of nineteenth-century Hulme, the grid of streets, the sandstone schoolhouses and the pubs. Luckily, there were also a few isolated pockets of good housing, houses with front doors and back gardens, along with some fine low-rise pre-war social housing built before the terrible experiment.

The hardest part of our job was to fashion an optimal social and community structure in this devastated district. One thing that gave us hope was that the rest of Manchester was already changing. The city center, only a quarter of a mile away but cut off by a motorway, was coming to life. New office buildings and the renovated canal district of Castlefield were just to the north, and an attractive parkway entrance to the city from the airport, running right through Hulme, was stimulating business investment. Immediately to the east was the largest concentration of post-secondary institutions outside of London, clustered around the University of Manchester. All of this energy could be used to break Hulme out from its physical and social isolation.

As in so many cities, large-scale public ownership of urban land had removed Hulme from the organic processes of growth and change happening all around it. Our plan aimed to fracture the borders around this huge parcel of land by creating physical and transit links and bridges to that healthier urban tissue, opening Hulme to the city around it, allowing ordinary urban activities to occur incrementally, not catastrophically. Exposure to the larger city would help to heal its culture of poverty and dependence. We favored small blocks, a diversity of uses, a variety of employment and living opportunities. It was all very Jane Jacobs, as Moses clearly had failed. As so many former council tenants had already voted with their feet and moved on, the number of people to be rehoused after demolition was manageable. We wanted to give them the choice of buying houses and flats or renting from a variety of housing and social organizations. The scale of housing management had to be kept small so that no single owner or agency could drag the entire district down if their block failed. Competition over housing management acts to everyone's benefit. The mix of tenancy and ownership (a hard ideological battle when we started) was, we felt, essential to permit social dynamism. Members of the community who become better off must be able to buy property in their neighborhood. When they stay, they provide the income and drive to maintain good schools and social services, to become the people who know how to complain effectively when things go bad.

We produced the basic physical plan for the new Hulme with a few months of chaotic, concentrated work. I had terrible doubts about our proposals. It must be remembered that these design ideas were once quite novel, especially in England where architects, then modernists to a man, disdained Jane Jacobs, as most still do. Also, if experience with Hulme had taught me anything it is how dangerous it is to apply a single concept to a large piece of city. I asked myself if anyone was really qualified to plan on this scale if we had not simply replaced the bold zeal of modernism with a cloying, nostalgic urban village straight out of Prince Charles's imagination. We produced a fully rendered, cut-foam model. As we presented the model to the client, Sir Alan Cockshaw, I wanted to tell him to throw it away, that we really did not know what we were doing. Instead, he literally nailed it to the wall of the project boardroom and told everyone this is exactly what he wanted. He pretty much got it: our vision as realized by a multitude of capable individuals, foremost among them the fine Manchester architect George Mills.

Hulme, now twenty years old, was the first comprehensive council housing estate remake in the U.K. in a model that has now become the accepted style for urban regeneration around the world. The strategy of demolishing, diversifying, and densifying large mid-century estates, of normalizing the street patterns, of mixing uses and activities, of connecting to the surrounding city is now standard practice. In Toronto, it can be seen most effectively in the remaking of the Regent Park and Alexandra Park estates. It demonstrates the pre-eminence of good planning over architecture, confirming that you cannot trust architects with an urban problem of any scale or seriousness. They will always go for a bigger, shinier idea. Although the on-the-ground reality of Hulme differs in many ways from our early plan, it is in all essentials exactly what we intended, and it is one of the places I feel proudest of on revisiting. What's more, it meets Jacobs' clear test for a healthy neighborhood in that it has provoked positive change in all surrounding areas.

* * *

I became the master planner for Hulme because of another phone call. Howard Bernstein asked me if I would do the re-planning. Or, rather, he told me I would do it. Now appropriately Sir Howard, he is the maker of modern Manchester and, arguably, the best big city manager in the world, having been either deputy or chief executive of the city since the mid-eighties until his retirement in 2017. He started work for the city in the Clerks Department at the age of seventeen and never worked anywhere else. Fond of big risks, he thinks on a grand scale and employs a close, inscrutable management style that somehow allows him to give appropriate attention to every detail without ever losing touch of the larger strategy. With a strong sense of Manchester's history, he likes to remind you that he did not invent the place—he simply resuscitated it. His Victorian predecessors were always undertaking ambitious urban projects, building the ship canal to bypass Liverpool, seizing a central place in the emerging rail network and constructing their magnificent Town Hall, a true civic cathedral. He just rediscovered their vision and competence. It was the intervening decades of municipal emasculation, bureaucratization, and timidity that were the aberration. *The Times* recently ranked Sir Howard as one of the most powerful people in the U.K. I do not know any of the others, but he certainly impresses me.

Sir Howard Bernstein presents, from first meeting, as a unique man, slight and Napoleonic with a compelling brow, a slick of black hair. I always picture him walking with short steps through the Gothic corridors of the Town Hall, dressed in black, scarf tight around his neck, head down, hands thrust into his pockets. He conveys an intimidating force and then suddenly his head rises, his eyes sparkle, he smiles and takes the arm or shoulder of someone he has met. "Hello mate, hello darling." He particularly brightens in the presence of smart women, with whom he increasingly surrounded himself. Fond of capable people, beloved by his generals, except for those he posted in distant suburbs, Sir Howard is the only client I have who frightens me. Not physically. I worry that I will not meet his expectations. I cannot bullshit him. He is a tough Manchester lad, through and through. Raised in the Jewish neighborhood north of the center, he has a Star of David as big as a knuckle-duster on his ring finger. His diet was something out of those back streets. When we had quick lunches during the bombing reconstruction, I would grab a bap (Manchester for sandwich) from around the corner while he would consume a Mars bar, a can of coke and a particular brand of potato rings, followed by a cigar. On that solid foundation modern Manchester was built.

Unlike Robert Moses, Sir Howard never aspired to combine his civil power with political power. His city council leaders were always his ultimate bosses and he was blessed throughout his reign by unusual continuity on that political level. He worked with two long-serving and impressive council leaders (effectively mayors, in North American parlance), Graham Stringer and Sir Richard Leese, the latter spanning the two decades after the bomb. That stability and his good relations with his elected colleagues have been keys to his success, along with a reputation for incorruptibility built over innumerable, complex projects for which he had complete authority.

In his capacity as Manchester's municipal entrepreneur, a role he invented for himself, Sir Howard undertook enormous infrastructure projects that would curl the hair of most city administrators. Of course, all of them cost money and that is where his strategic genius was most evident. U.K. cities have minimal taxing powers: 94 per cent of their income comes from the national government. So Bernstein always ensured that Manchester was best positioned to take advantage of any new national or European funding program or to secure pieces of national megaprojects such as the high-speed rail line north from London, customarily receiving the first and largest tranche of whatever public funding was available. He also leveraged the city's assets to great effect. He packaged dead, city-owned land and buildings and transferred them *en bloc* to joint ventures with sovereign fund investors in exchange for mixed-income rental housing commitments. He has married key institutions such as the university and Manchester City Football Club to big spenders from the Emirates. His handling of the Manchester-owned airport asset was breathtaking: he sold a succession of shares, used the proceeds to acquire other U.K. airports, such as London's Stanstead, and then refinanced the collective assets to fund further expansions while producing a healthy dividend for Town Hall. It is the gift that keeps on growing and giving.

As importantly, he inserted Manchester's voice into every national debate, be it about airports, rail networks or housing policy. Backing him in all of these ventures was New Economy Manchester, his seventy-person, in-house, strategic consulting group, for my money the most effective organization of its kind, doing much of the heavy lifting behind Howard's big moves. One file that is now showing fruition is an ambitious plan to devolve the delivery of health and social services from the national to the local level under the wonderful soubriquet of "DevoMax." Howard is convinced that it will deliver huge efficiencies and quality improvements. To properly receive the new powers, he spent his last years in office building the basis of a regional urban government, with Manchester at the heart of a ten-municipality city region. A new regional city mayor was voted into office in 2017, just as Howard finally retired.

His initiatives are always pursued aggressively and collaboratively rather than antagonistically. Bernstein likes to set up senior levels of government with perfect passes so they can put the ball in the net themselves, pose for the cameras, and take the glory. It does not matter to him which team wins: he will work with whatever party is in office. Similarly, Manchester's Labour city council was just as happy to pass to Margaret Thatcher as to Tony Blair or David Cameron. George Osborne, the former Conservative Chancellor of the Exchequer became Sir Howard's close friend. Osborne, interestingly, was convinced of the necessity of empowering city governments in the Robert Moses style by a reading of Robert Caro's *The Power Broker*.

Not all of Bernstein's plans work perfectly. At his insistence, Manchester advanced the concept of a northern powerhouse, with itself at the hub of a group of northern cities including Liverpool, Leeds and Sheffield, all tied together with infrastructure investments to create the critical mass for a globally competitive megacity. Despite that vision, Manchester's economy is still worryingly underpowered and fighting the winner-take-all trends of the contemporary global economy. Unlike North America, or indeed much of Europe, where several secondary cities have shown remarkable economic independence, regional Manchester, amounting to a single municipality the size of Los Angeles, is overpowered by London. Even with people and businesses fleeing the capital because of high housing prices, office rents and an impossible cost of living, Manchester is finding it difficult to achieve that megacity status. There is a nagging worry that the new high-speed rail link to London will act as a drain of economic activity rather than a spigot.

* * *

Manchester was one of the few places in the country outside of London that wanted to stay in the EU, not surprisingly since more than half of its traded goods are exported. It is now at risk from that bone-headed Brexit vote. All the more reason for the city to aggressively open up new economic sectors. The relocation of a large chunk of the BBC to MediaCity in Salford has given a boost to the digital economy, spawning an impressive cluster of TV and film initiatives, and more could follow as the media economy is increasingly resistant to London's high operating and labor costs. Manchester has made some daring innovations in new space creation to accommodate that industry, creating The Sharp Project, a converted former TV factory that offers cheap, cheerful short-term and long-term work space focusing on media, all in shipping container offices surrounded by pool and ping-pong tables and a café. The game-changing graphene story is just beginning, with massive investments in a new graphene center at the university intended to facilitate the new semi-metal's transition from scientific discovery to entrepreneurial breakthrough. And on top of all this is the one field, or pitch, in which Manchester's ambition to become the world's leading post-industrial city is most dramatically demonstrated: the Manchester City Football Academy.

The Football Academy is where the game of football, a tradition of working-class life in the U.K.'s industrial cities, is being re-invented. On the sprawling site of a former chemical works in east Manchester, an industrial-scale factory for the production of skilled soccer players has been created. The academy has sixteen outdoor pitches, a 7,000-seat stadium for the women's team and men's A team, and a vast indoor pitch built to FIFA World Cup standards. Room and board are provided for fifty young trainees, as well as top-of-the-line accommodations for the first team before match days. Our firm created the first site plan sketches for the academy just five years before it went into full operation. Man City, benefitting from the sizeable capital infusions of its Abu Dhabi owner, Sheikh Mansour, can move at warp speed as part of his admirably megalomaniacal intent to become the leading soccer force in the world. He has already conquered Great Britain. His team is all but unbeatable. The theory of the academy seems to be that you find some talented Brazilian or Congolese street kid, bring him and his family, if need be, to Manchester, feed him broccoli and avocados for a couple of years, train him night and day and you will create a property worth several million pounds. The academy has only been open a few years, so it is too early to tell whether the business model works but judging by what I saw not all the valuable players come from away. On the indoor pitch about a hundred local eight-year-olds were practicing. Anyone of them could have run rings around me in my not-very-prime prime. The team is resolutely grooming this local talent. It would love to create a home-grown captain to help enhance the brand and convince the locals that Manchester City, not Manchester United, just the other side of the city center, is the real Manchester team. Man City/Man United. Yankees/Mets. Cubs/White Sox. Roma/Lazio. Rangers/Islanders. What a rush, a daily drama, for a city lucky enough to have two world-class teams in the same sport. What a time we would have in Toronto if we had another hockey team.

I have worked in Manchester for decades and I still do not know by what DNA a person makes their team selection between United and City. It is a secret code, an endless beer-fueled conversation. "You don't pick a team, it picks you," explains an otherwise intelligent man. Perhaps the teams are the Janus face of any city: the global brand, the home team. Whatever the rationale, there is no doubt that football has reached a critical mass in Manchester. Having two top rank teams, with two more just down the road in Liverpool, and a cluster of other Premier League clubs in the surrounding region proves that agglomeration economies work in sports as in other industries. If a player is released by one club, he can find another in the same commuter-shed. There is a fully developed infrastructure of agents, advisors and medical expertise, and an attractive sports culture that serves as a magnet for young Brazilian, Ukrainian, Nigerian and Portuguese talent. And the city-region is big and wealthy enough that football spouses can not only go shopping, they can get a good job. Sports are a huge component of the local economy.

It is the food served in the Academy that demonstrates the total transformation from the old world of football, the old Manchester. Its new incarnation is uncompromisingly healthy. Today's mains: chickpea and cauliflower salad and a Mediterranean couscous with roasted vegetables. What is not on the menu? Chips, baked beans, sausage, bacon, black pudding, fried eggs, fried bread, muffins, custard, scampi, soft drinks. Hard drinks, liquor, even beer—all of the football food and drink that fueled players in my youth is gone. The global football machine has taken over the game's diet. Delightfully re-invented, like the city.

7

BELFAST –
NOBODY KNOWS
MY TROUBLES

The first meeting with Belfast's chief executive was in a London hotel. A man in a hurry, about to retire in six months, he wanted a plan for his city center. He knew nothing about city planning, he explained, so he had phoned Sir Howard Bernstein in Manchester who had recommended us. There would have to be some kind of selection process but would we do it?

The reason he claimed to know nothing about planning, disingenuously, of course, is where this Belfast story begins. Early in The Troubles, as the more than three decades of deadly sectarian strife in Northern Ireland are known, Belfast had all of its planning, housing and regeneration powers removed by the British government. Some of the authorities are considered to have discriminated against the Roman Catholic minority, restricting access to jobs, housing, and community facilities. Through the 1970s and 1980s, the city was home to a low-grade civil war with much of the violence—shootings, beatings, bombings—concentrated in the tight working-class neighborhoods surrounding the city center. In the nineties, a struggling momentum towards peace finally culminated in the Good Friday Accords that, through elaborate power-sharing structures, returned democratic government to the province from British trusteeship. One of those accords returned city planning and development powers back to Belfast City Council. We were called a year before it was to be finalized. Could the chief executive have a plan, please? I noticed during our breakfast, which was held in a private room, that every time a server came through the door our host and his colleague fell silent. They started up again when the server left. I got a sense that this might not be an ordinary job.

Our firm specializes in planning downtowns, waterfronts and similar large-scale urban projects. We know what to expect when we start. A huge pile of reports, previous plans, by-laws, regulations and so on. Belfast would be the first time we had worked in a major city without any such heap of relevant and irrelevant paper. It had not done any planning for two decades. "Doesn't matter. It's really quite simple," the chief executive explained. "Tell me the five things I should do in the city center, tell me why, and tell me how." Who could ask for a better brief?

First impressions are so important, travelling new to a city. You remember what you see, what you feel, the sense of the place, the colors, the sounds or lack thereof. The buildings, the taxi drivers, the streets, the hotel clerks, restaurant servers, trees and parks and people. Especially in my business, you can quickly learn too much about a city, all the reasons why and why not. So it helps to dwell on first impressions, to imagine yourself a tourist, an investor, an immigrant or a kid from the sticks. What kind of place is this? Am I going to like it? Is it beautiful? Does it work? Does it leave me curious for more? In what way is it, or could it be, perfect?

I always write down my first impressions. Here is Belfast.

A grand and handsome city, an imperial city, like Liverpool, Glasgow and Cardiff. A capital city, although it's not quite clear of what. Its bones are Victorian; a magnificently extravagant neo-classical City Hall right at the center with shining white limestone turrets and pergolas. Surrounded by a grid of fine buildings. Great green hills lean in from either side. Giant yellow ship-building cranes with oil rigs under construction mark the way to the sea. In the low spring evening light, the city softens. There's a bustle around the center but it fades quickly to the north, where the city gets harder, emptier, vacant. Nothing worse than many other northern U.K. and European cities but empty lots, too much asphalt, not enough trees. The river, the city's reason for being, is a place apart, edged by a last round of waterfront development but lacking any visual or activity interest. It's a compact center, that's good. You can walk across it in fifteen minutes. But it is also a detached center, separated from the surrounding residential areas by a ring of expressways, rail tracks and the river. Still, it's in much better shape than I had expected. It doesn't look or feel like a war zone.

Good money has been spent on fine streetscaping and a couple of key buildings, an interesting arts center and a well-executed in-city shopping center complex—a difficult urban trick to execute. New office buildings—a very good sign—but on the edge, not in the center. It's clean, no litter. The extensive stock of heritage buildings has been well maintained. But the active center is too small for the city it is. Retail looks in big trouble, with too many vacancies. The few recent apartment buildings stare dead-eyed at the river. Everyone who works here seems to be gone by 5 p.m. Not enough life, liveliness, people, cars, residents, shoppers, workers, tourists. There's a hip district, the Cathedral Quarter, but the bars and restaurants are quiet after 9 p.m. If anybody lives here, it isn't obvious. Not enough activity. Not enough green. Not enough business. We'll have to see what we can do about all that.

Through the decades of The Troubles, over 3,500 people were killed and tens of thousands were injured. The number of fatalities is slightly higher than the total of 9/11 in New York, in a city less than one-twelfth the size. That the deaths were spread over decades rather than hours makes for a different sort of disaster, and a different sort of trauma, but disaster and trauma nonetheless. Everyone in Northern Ireland has a close and bitter experience of The Troubles. So many terrible things were done by all involved. People have long memories but these, thankfully, have not prevented everyone from engaging in a genuine search for peace in recent years, a project requiring impressive, relentless citizenship and studied generosity at both the personal and political levels. For these were mostly "neighborly murders," in poet Seamus Heaney's chilling phrase. That is why there is so much riding on these halting steps towards a permanent peace.

One consequence of The Troubles is that the neighborhoods surrounding Belfast's center, which used to be quite mixed, have become more homogenous, with Catholics and Protestants fenced into their own districts. Literally fenced in. At the worst of the violence, "peace walls" segregated the neighborhoods into homogenous communities and they remain in place, just in case. Imagine a fifteen-meter-high chain link fence in New York's Lower Manhattan between Little Italy and Chinatown, between the Jewish and Bangladeshi sections of Shoreditch in London, or in Toronto between Italian College Street and Portuguese Dundas Street, each enclave decorated with vast murals depicting the saints and martyrs of their cause. About thirty kilometers of fencing still exists, winding its way around each sectarian pocket, although for several years now, as tensions have abated, the armed gates between the sections have been opened and the fences are slowly being disassembled.

These sectarian neighborhoods were directly affected by the collapse of Belfast's traditional shipbuilding, engineering and linen mill economies. Although these industries disappeared thirty or more years ago, the culture of manual labor, the notion that real work requires dirty hands and a concomitant disdain for education persist, particularly in the Protestant communities. Employment discrimination against Catholics had ironically encouraged them to upgrade their skills. In stark contrast to the brilliant educational achievements of the better parts of Belfast, only 3 per cent of the children in the worst areas further their educations after high school. A hard nut of the undereducated, unemployed and unemployable exists in all comparable northern European cities, but these people can get up to a lot more trouble in Northern Ireland.

The recession of 2008–2009 hit Northern Ireland hard, worse than the mainland U.K. Its biggest trading partner, the Irish Republic, less than an hour to the south, suffered an almost fatal business, banking and property collapse. When we arrived several years later, house values had yet to regain their pre-recession levels on both sides of the border but things were looking up. It seemed as though a new knowledge-based business was relocating or expanding in the north every week, bringing another 50, 100 or 200 employees. There was a critical shortage of office space, just the kind of problem we like to have. With an unemployment rate well over the U.K. national average, every possible new job for the region was coaxed with generous and sophisticated incentives. The machine had to be revived, even if it was force fed. Peace in the province is highly dependent on prosperity.

By the time we arrived, one big addition to Belfast's economic machine was already having remarkable consequences. Titanic Belfast opened in 2012, a major tourist attraction featuring historical and interactive exhibits on the very site at which the great, tragic ocean liner was constructed. Its continuing success has given a big boost to the city's confidence. The Titanic Quarter in which the attraction is located is also home to the studios in which *Game of Thrones* is created. The popular series has made a star of the extraordinary landscapes of Northern Ireland where much of the filming occurs. Another unexpected tourism boost came from the art of The Troubles, the extraordinary tribal murals found throughout the inner city. As the bitterness that prompted these works fades, what was once violent, righteous propaganda is steadily transmuted into cultural content for mass consumption. If that is not peace, I don't know what is. Belfast's tourism numbers, especially for out-of-province visitors, are impressive and, apparently, durable.

* * *

Our project meetings were held in the chief executive's grand office in the City Hall, complete with huge windows, fireplace and marble columns. It is a veritable copy of Sir Howard Bernstein's room in Manchester. These Victorian city builders thought well of themselves. On the wall, on the mantelpiece and on the shelves are a dense clutter of memorabilia of the type seen in all municipal leaders' offices, except here one finds a personal note from Barack and Michelle, some trinkets left by Bill and Hillary, and a signed poem from Seamus Heaney. That a damp, mid-size city on the north-east coast of Ireland merits such attention speaks to both the magnitude of Belfast's problems and the sincerity of the world's hope for its lasting peace.

We arranged meetings with everyone we could: city officials, agencies, developers, arts groups, retailers, lobbyists, community leaders, activists, editors, people with ideas, interests, obsessions. We inhaled Belfast, hour after hour. It was fascinating. Wonderful, richly imaginative, deeply committed people live in the city, and love the city, and can they talk! This may be the North, but it is Ireland, after all. Words rush at you like white water. We try not to form any conclusions, just ask questions and listen. Let people have their say, give them the time they need to tell you what they feel you really need to know. The trick to being a good city planner, as with a happy marriage, is to be a little bit deaf. At least half of what you hear from these kinds of meetings is nonsense. The skill is in knowing which half.

We also walked. We walked every block, at all times of day and night, to fix the feel of the city under our feet. And we studied the facts. Markets, costs, demographics, economics, traffic statistics. These awkward facts are what distinguish real urban planning from activist advocacy. Not all things are possible. There are choices.

It was clear to us early on that the plan was going to have to be about people and their prospects, not just physical projects. A working relationship was established early with the University of Ulster, which was in the process of moving its large main campus into the northern part of the center, becoming probably the most effective instrument of change for the entire area. Educational and institutional connections to surrounding neighborhoods could challenge the culture of worklessness and raise aspiration and ambition in youth and the unemployed. Every post-industrial country in the developed world is trying to tackle this problem: it is what produces Brexit, Donald Trump, Marie le Pen, and the Ford brothers. But in places the modern economy has left behind, nobody really knows what to do.

The first presentation of our initial directions was held in the Emergency Room, a large boardroom with chalkboards, telephones and monitors, with a couple of secure rooms off to the side. Happily, it has not had to deal with many recent emergencies, although sudden violent clashes persist over symbolic issues: how many days a year can the Union Jack fly over City Hall, and the routes of loyalist parades. Absurd to an outsider, but tenaciously resistant to resolution. Our committee consisted of the leaders of the six political parties on city council. Belfast's ranked balloting system is designed to give voice to a plethora of parties including, at the moment, Sinn Fein and the Socialist Democratic Labour Party (both Republican), three Unionist parties, and a centrist party, all in a city of half a million. Most of the councilors looked like municipal politicians the world over, slightly rumpled, slightly harried, although a couple were quite distinct—large muscled men with polished scalps and trim goatees, men with hard history in The Troubles. All settled into the room. The Republican joshes the unionist: "Was in East Belfast [the unionist stronghold] last week. Ya murals now, they're not up to scratch. Getting formulaic, so it is." The unionist lowered his jaw. "Right you are. The quality, the human touch, not there anymore. Computer design is it now. No feeling in it." They both shake their heads in dismay and we proceed to discuss parks and public art. Peace through urban design.

We suggested strategies for new office and housing districts in the city's center, and for reversing the retail slide. Belfast does not have a typical central shopping district. For almost thirty years, the center was ringed by a security fence. Everyone entering was subject to an airport-style search, not the best way to build customer loyalty. Given the active competition from out-of-town retail options, it is surprising that there is a functioning city center at all. We also advocated a general softening and greening of the city. The street system was to be calmed and simplified. The river, cut off to the east, was to be brought back into the heart of the city. Strong transit connections were recommended to tie troubled surrounding districts to the success of the core, along with a major new park to knit the new university complex into the center. There was general acceptance of where we were headed.

It all seemed a bit too easy. And then Gerry Adams, the leader of Sinn Fein, was arrested for questioning in connection with a particularly hideous terrorist murder early in The Troubles. The ground shook for four days. Republicans condemned dark political forces. "Up yours," said the Unionists. Positions hardened.

It is easy to get carried away with the prospects for peace in Northern Ireland. Everyone comes to Belfast with good intentions, including all the politicians with their trinkets. A friend recounted a meeting in which a delegation of Toronto non-profit foundations earnestly lectured Belfast's feuding parties on our city's long tradition of getting along. "Have you ever killed a man?" asked one of the locals at the table. Toronto did not know how to respond. The city's peace or, rather, its lack of conflict, is fragile and dependent to a large extent on what Tony Blair and Bill Clinton, chief architects of the 1997 accord, characterized as "creative ambiguity." It requires a determination to forego, at least for the moment, the investigation of past wrongs in order to forge ahead. Is that justice? Tough question. But it is the only way forward. Adams was released without charge, relieving the tension as quickly as it had come on. Of course, it will never really be over.

My son, who knows Belfast, phoned me with advice: "Remember Dad, you're just a plumber, not the Dalai Lama." So planner, plumber, what are we actually going to do?

The City organized a public presentation of our final report. They wanted everyone in the room. Cities that have something bold to do cannot be led by their formal government alone. They need a broader constituency representing the whole of the body politic, the great and the good, business, arts and academic leaders, community organizers. I saw it happen in Manchester after the bombing. New York Mayors Giuliani and Bloomberg both convened similar estates general after 9/11 and the Wall Street crash, and something similar occurred in Toronto after the SARS crisis when the Summit Alliance, convened by the redoubtable management consultant David Pecaut, forced a bold agenda of action on a hapless city council. Belfast is lucky because, unlike larger cities, it can assemble all key stakeholders under one reasonably sized roof. It is a huge advantage for a city seeking the consensus essential to moving a big agenda forward.

Before going public, the review committee wanted to have a last look at things. There was a lot of pressure to include more social housing in the mix. It is a standard request from politicians and community leaders, all the more so in a divided city where control over housing means control over votes. They suspected that I wanted to fill their city center with yuppies. They could have been right. It is one of those times when it helps to be from away. Belfast is the rare city that does not need more affordable housing. It is not London or Sydney or any other booming global city. It already has the cheapest housing in the U.K. and its worst central neighborhoods are emptying as residents vote with their feet. You can buy a terrace house for less than $100,000. Nor does it need more poor people. It has concentrations of the lowest incomes and least employment in the country. It needs more people with money in their pocket, more wealth, more jobs, more economic activity. It needs fuel for the machine. If we can attract more well-paid knowledge workers to live, work, shop, eat and sip cappuccinos in the center of Belfast and spread those opportunities to the surrounding neighborhoods we will call it success. "Just more trickle-down nonsense," say the housing activists. Maybe, but trickle-up does not seem to have worked here. You have to have something to redistribute.

This debate between the city as an agent of wealth creation or the city as a promoter of wealth redistribution has gone global. It is particularly acute in Europe where the combination of slow recovery from the recession and frail public finances have put into question the affordability and effectiveness of the income safety nets and housing support programs that characterize social democracies. It is also increasingly clear that contemporary urban economies are inherently "spiky," to use urban analyst Richard Florida's adjective. It disproportionately rewards the talented while abandoning the unskilled. You can have economic growth or you can have income equality. What seems difficult is to have both in a world in which cities as much as countries or companies are fiercely competitive. For Belfast, this left/right debate, obscured for decades by the sectarian divide, might be the foundation of a new political culture. Frankly, that would be a great step forward.

Through all the consultation, I slowly pick up distinctions between the factions, if only about body types. The Republicans run to string beans, the loyalists to fire plugs. The Republicans have a dangerous charm, over-confident that history and poetry are on their side. The unionists, sure of right and might, have a stubborn fortitude, with a hint of Trump. Stereotypes of course, but somewhat true. The reality is that there are many other differences in dress, dialect and demeanor that would take years of close study for an outsider to master. What is abundantly clear is that both sides are quick to default to grievance and finger-pointing. Both sides have deep wells of resentment on which to draw. At one point we do a word count to make sure we have the same number of "wests" and "easts" in the final report. Regardless, I like these people. Even the tension has an endearing side, the complete opposite of Toronto's often passive-aggressive style. In a Belfast meeting you will be hit in the face by a series of verbal sucker punches. Afterwards, you will get a hug and a Guinness.

* * *

It is not surprising, given the way they use language, that the Northern Irish have taken to ice hockey. The game has become another route to peace and reconciliation in Belfast. The Belfast Giants deliberately organized themselves as a non-sectarian team, banning particular national anthems, colors, flags and even soccer shirts of teams like Glasgow Rangers or Celtic who draw Protestant and Catholic supporters respectively. They have a large and enthusiastic non-sectarian fan base composed largely of teenage girls who, apparently, come for the music. The Giants have been a great success with the help of several National Hockey League stars, good Canadian names from a few years back including Theo Fleury, Jason Bowen and Paxton Schulte.

Despite a shared love of hockey, it would be hard to conceive of two cities more different than Belfast and Toronto. One old world, one new. One grand, one utilitarian. One barely ticking over, one growing like crazy. And, of course, one tribal, one famously post-tribe. Belfast is 96 per cent white. Forget about Catholics and Protestants: that is the critical urban statistic. Toronto had troubles of its own until time and massive immigration buried the old tensions. It was once the largest Orange town in the world. Every mayor of Toronto since its founding was an Orangeman until Nathan Philips, a fine Jewish mayor, was elected in 1954. Even our current mayor, John Tory, draws his name from a bunch of brigands and Royalist cattle thieves in the Irish back-country. The Orange Lodge has now faded away but it left a strong trace in Toronto's DNA. An unostentatious blandness, a distrust of beauty, an enduring politeness and personal generosity, a relentless localism, a love of domesticity, a pleasing reserve, a reticence regarding sex. It favors peace, order and government, and don't get too big for yourself.

One of the fascinating aspects of Toronto is the way these traits seem consistently passed on to new generations as they arrive from all over the world. The Ulster aristocracy rests eternal in the names of the Toronto school system. I recently took my granddaughter to the finals of the city's middle school volleyball competition at Duke of Connaught School in Leslieville, a gentrifying inner-east district. About a third of the girls wore headscarves, about a third were white, the rest everything under the sun. All of them whip-smart, fit, polite and smiling. All of them Torontonians in a manner that the old Orange city would recognize. Duke of Connaught, Earl Haig, Earl Grey, Earl Kitchener, Lord Dufferin, Lord Lansdowne. Is that how our distinct cultural character endures, transmitted through those ennobled public school names, bricks and mortar? Is there nothing so permanent as culture, in cities as in people?

Nothing in city planning happens fast and our six months in Belfast stretch to a year. There are a few political wobbles. A fifth urban "quarter" has to be added to the original four in our plan. So be it. This is not the time to be precious about math. It is their plan now, not ours. An energetic female chief executive, Suzanne Wylie, takes over, one of a fine tribe of strong-shouldered Northern Irish women steadily replacing the embattled males. That has to be progress. The plan is unanimously adopted by the city council. There will be further consultations, of course, but Belfast has agreed on its future. Just in time for the Brexit vote, which threatens to change the game in significant ways, opening all the old questions. Ambiguity about the status of Northern Ireland worked remarkably well in the past, but those days seem over. Unification with the Republic might now make sense to most citizens. Certainly, a hard border with Europe in the middle of Ireland will make none.

After all this hard work we repair to a savior of a place, Mourne's Seafood Bar, tucked into a back street north of City Hall. It is a black-paneled, wood table kind of bar, always packed. Even using all of the influence of City Hall, both Sinn Fein and Unionist, we find it tough to get seated. Great oysters from Galway. Really fresh fish on the bone—is there anything so sweet? As it relates to fish, fresh is the difference between heaven and blotting paper.

I have a theory that good food is the leading indicator of urban regeneration. Restaurants are pioneer businesses, first in where others will not go. More importantly, the act of eating good food in the company of strangers is perhaps the quintessential urban activity, a mélange of conviviality and curiosity that speaks well for the future of any neighborhood. The same instincts that argue for a satisfying city also argue for a good and companionable meal, and inspire great cooks to create them. You can eat well in Belfast now and the food has no sectarian taste. Better yet, it has a local taste, a post-conflict taste, from Belfast's own fields, its own seas. There is a great market, recently voted the best in Britain, with a full range of mass and artisanal producers. It is my kind of food. Well-hung beef and lamb, fresh fish, root vegetables, dark greens, full-flavored beer, solid bread, cheese with a serious back story. Duck, pheasant, rabbit, venison, eels. Stews, roasts, grills and pottage to keep the climate at bay. A unique culinary delight.

Belfast is not perfect by any standard definition. It is a dance of three steps forward and two steps back. But social resilience, getting back on your feet and learning how to live together after all that violence, these are skills that are perhaps better developed in Belfast than in any other once-devastated city. Belfast stands proud like a late-round boxer, having absorbed more than a few hits but still with a swagger and a force that makes you take note. As visiting Canadians, we are innocent observers of the city's drama. Deliberate innocents. It is one of the advantages of our nationality and we use it. We are not the English with their attitude, the Irish with their baggage, the Europeans with their effortless certainty, the Americans with their bombast. Being nice and harmless is an effective business strategy. We do get along, and perhaps we helped a little too, being from away, having experience of a starkly different flow of life, notwithstanding our similar roots. And after a drink or two, we recite a poem, that hopeful Heaney poem on the chief executive's wall. And another drink please, because we have a long journey to make, back to Toronto, the town to which Belfast in many ways gave birth.

> History says, Don't hope
> On this side of the grave,
> But then, once in a lifetime
> The longed-for tidal wave
> Of justice can rise up
> And hope and history rhyme.
>
> *The Cure at Troy*
> Seamus Heaney

8

TORONTO –
THE ACCIDENTAL
METROPOLIS

Every year I start my graduate class at the University of Toronto planning school with an exercise on city rankings. Comparative ratings of cities are much the media fashion—I dump about fifty on my students, ranking everything from stock market power to mobile phone usage, gay-friendliness to airport connectivity. The wonk in me wants to foster their suspicion of such indices by examining the often flimsy methodology they employ, but the urban traveler in me wants them to listen carefully to the song these sirens are singing. The rankings are individually suspect but collectively they say a lot about what is going on in the world's cities. I ask the students what story the rankings tell about Toronto. I get two reactions: shock, followed by disbelief.

Shock, because by evidence of comparisons with other world cities, Toronto is a huge success, a city that scores highly on the soundness of its finance, tech and business sectors and on the quality of its social, community and cultural life. There are, as the range of rankings show, endless ways to assess a city's success but Toronto is regularly in the top five in the world for its livability and culture, in the top ten for its

financial services, international accessibility, creativity and innovation, and in the top twenty for its business clout. Various analysts
have tried combining these measures into a composite index of urban
significance. Depending on how they weight the numbers, Toronto
generally lands between sixth and sixteenth place as most significant
city in the world.

The numbers cannot lie—well, individually they might but taken
together they tell a clear story of Toronto's sudden global prominence,
inducing in my students, as well as in the general city public, that
second reaction of disbelief—almost horror—because this story is profoundly at odds with the city's self-narrative. Torontonians see Toronto
as a place of inadequacy, unimportance, incompetence and inequity. It
is an ugly, expensive, second-rate town. Its aspirations to a world-class
status are preposterous.

Which raises two fascinating questions: how did this no-account
dorp become globally significant? And why is Toronto's self-image so
at war with its actual status?

Outside observers of the city are often struck by these apparent con-
tradictions. One global urban analyst recently commented that Toronto
is the only world city whose publicly promoted stories about itself are
less impressive than its reality. Which is something of a relief, given that
the world of urbanism is over-filled with boosterism. To be at a global
cities conference is to be in a room with a herd of Michelin men, their
inflated civic personas bouncing off each other. Toronto stands apart.
"The biggest city in the world nobody's ever heard of," according to
a speaker at one such European conference. Toronto's reticence flows
from the core of its psyche. It is bred in its Belfast, Scotch-Irish bones.
It is a city where, unlike every other place in which I have worked, the
phrase "world class'" is used as a negative epithet, denoting hubristic
self-promotion.

Only two cities that were not economically significant a century ago
have since joined the global premier league: Singapore and Toronto. We
have seen the deliberate intent that propelled Singapore to greatness.
Not so Toronto. Unlike the rest of the world, no one in government,
even at the city level, has ever had any intention or strategy to make

it a global star. Quite the contrary. At the federal level, politicians have made a national sport of puncturing the city's modest pretensions. Conscious ignorance of Toronto has been a consistent theme of national politics. In my only encounter with Stephen Harper, shortly before he became prime minister, he flatly dismissed any prospect of Toronto becoming a global city. Harper is as awkwardly miserable a man as you could meet but what he forthrightly expressed is consistent with the views of his predecessors of all parties. A word count of the record of parliamentary debates gives a good indication of Canada's inattention to urban affairs. In 2015, grain transportation was mentioned more than public transportation, fish farming more than air pollution and the dairy industry twice as often as food banks. Of course, dismissiveness of urban affairs was historically supported by the nation's reliance on its oil, resource and agricultural industries, which provided jobs in a majority of constituencies. But that was then. The rapid retreat of oil and gas, the decline of commodity prices, global competition in agriculture, along with Trump's trade and tariff threats to those sectors have greatly weakened the traditional pillars of the Canadian economy. There is an increasing realization, confirmed by the election of Prime Minister Justin Trudeau at the head of the most urban-friendly government Canada has ever seen, that cities are Canada's future. And although the national accounts are harder to disentangle than those in the U.K., the Toronto region increasingly picks up the bills for the rest of the country.

Every other global city in which I have worked produces glossy documents full of confidently assertive strategies for advancing its world standing. Toronto is the only one I know that has never had a plan for becoming a global city, let alone for staying on top. Yet the rise of Toronto is now impossible to ignore, and it is irrepressibly gathering strength. One man might help explain why. Richard Florida is not your conventional academic. He is a successful writer, a sought-after speaker and an industrial-strength urban researcher. He has produced three excellent, simple ideas about the way modern cities work. His first and well-known observation documented the rise of what he calls the "creative class," demonstrating that the economies of cities are no longer driven directly by manufacturing or financial companies, or by business or media organizations, but by the innovative talents of the individuals who work in those enterprises: the creative class. The city that attracts, nurtures and rewards that class will be a success. Creative, innovative, entrepreneurial, energetic, well-educated people are what make successful cities. People first, and the place in which they want to live, before businesses, institutions or governments.

Florida moved to Toronto about a decade ago to join the Martin Prosperity Institute at the University of Toronto. Although he lives the life of an international academic, the confidante of mayors and ministers the world over, and maintains a parallel professorship at NYU, he has made Toronto home for his family. He does not look like a conventional academic as he dances free-mic'ed around a presentation stage in front of massive screens of data. A native of New Jersey, he hints of Travolta and Springsteen. Full of enthusiasm and projects, he is also full of affection for Toronto, something the city's pinched psyche often seems to have a hard time reciprocating. He knows everyone and does not give a shit. At our first meeting we name drop for a quarter of an hour. I search for any he cannot trump me on, finding only one. Trump himself.

So what is it, I ask him, that has made Toronto such a success? If it is not urban policy, large-scale infrastructure investment, good management or national urban sympathy—all those strategies employed by other aspirant cities being largely absent here—what is it that has propelled us to the urban elite? "Quite simply," he says, "it's immigration. Embrace the world's about-to-be best and brightest, and you will make your city." This might sound trendy, but it is an echo of ancient wisdom. Confucius, when asked what makes a good city, replied, "Keep local citizens happy and attract people from afar."

When I arrived in Toronto in the late 1960s, the most common names in the phone book were Smith, Brown, McLean and Cohen. A long-suffering grad student counted them again in the last printed phone book, issued in 2010, and the most frequent names were Lee, Wong, Smith (in steep decline). Patel, Singh and Kim were rising steadily.

That dramatic change in the city's make-up, and the less obvious but more significant change in the city's fortunes, was a consequence of changes made in 1967 to the Federal Immigration Act, introduced by the current prime minister's father, which significantly increased the scale of immigration to Canada, eliminating the preference shown to white European immigrants, thus opening the country's doors to the world. At some time in the past few years the city broke through the 50/50 line, with more than half of its population being foreign-born and more self-identifying as members of a visible minority, allowing us to retire that awful term—or, perhaps, to apply it to whites.

To my knowledge, there has never been a large city in world history with this demographic make-up. London, New York, Miami and Los Angeles, each of which style themselves as the most cosmopolitan city in the world, have roughly a third of their populations foreign-born. Historically, perhaps the ancient cities of the Mediterranean—Constantinople, Venice or Alexandria—might have come close. In the modern era, Toronto stands significantly ahead of the world, and its diversity continues to grow. Between 100,000 and 125,000 new immigrants arrive in the Toronto region every year, by far the highest rate for any European or North American city. The two-thirds foreign-born city looks to be only ten years or so away.

In recent decades, the city has received between a third and a half of the nation's newcomers. Canada's immigration points system favors those with good work qualifications who are moving into their peak earning years, and is structured to admit families rather than individuals. Which is to say that Toronto's immigrants are distinct from those we encountered in the Bronx and Barking. They are less the urban precariat than a middle class in waiting, with the highest educational levels of any country's migrants, superior even to those of their Canadian-born contemporaries. Although initial entry into the labor market at a level commensurate with that skill set is challenging, and perhaps getting more so, the evidence suggests that immigrants on average successfully settle into their new homeland in five to ten years, and that their children are somewhat more successful than children of Canadian-born families. That is a huge simplification of a very complex process but it is probably because of this individual success, and because Canada's immigrants do not typically enter at the bottom of the market and compete with white, lower-income locals for low-paying jobs, that the country has largely avoided the immigration backlash so characteristic of other Western countries in the Brexit and Trump era. Our own populists, including the late, former Toronto mayor Rob Ford and his brother Doug, now premier of Ontario, tend to lead ethnically diverse voting groups. Indeed, the general acceptance of immigration makes Canada a complete outlier. A recent poll indicated that about 82 per cent of Canadians thought high levels of immigration made a positive economic contribution to the country, a number double that in the U.S., and several times that in the U.K. or Europe.

It is the sheer organic energy released by high-quality mass immigration that fuels the machine of modern Toronto, far more than any intentional policy, program or set of projects. About two decades ago an acute observer of Toronto, Robert Fulford, wrote what is still one of the best books on the city, *Accidental City*. It is from him that I stole the title of this chapter. Toronto has now matured to become an accidental metropolis because its unintended global ascent has been driven almost entirely by external forces, principally immigration. No one planned for this to happen. Toronto's complete lack of a self-advancement strategy may prove to be the most successful strategy of all.

Within the ever-flowing river of immigration there have nonetheless been important eddies, each sparked by some external event, each leaving its mark on the city. In 1956, the short-lived Hungarian revolution brought some 37,000 souls, mostly families, to Canada, and primarily to Toronto. A host of new Hungarian-led restaurants and businesses sprang up in the city. In the late 1960s, a flood of roughly 40,000 well-educated, ethically motivated young men refusing to join America's war in Vietnam swept into Toronto, changing its cultural scene forever. Even after the US granted them amnesty, about half remained. The largest migrant wave of all was, however, from within the country. After the election of the separatist Parti Québécois government in 1976, some 300,000 people, mostly Anglophones from Quebec's largest city, Montreal, drove down Highway 401 to Toronto, bringing a large chunk of the nation's financial, business and cultural life with them. The fall of Saigon directed about 50,000 Vietnamese boat people to the city. The dictatorship of Idi Amin, chaos in Eritrea, anarchy in Mogadishu, ethnic conflict in Sri Lanka, the implosion of the Balkans, clampdowns in Tibet, the heart-rending nightmare of Syria—each time the world convulses, some tens of thousands of newcomers appear in Toronto's streets.

What the numbers obscure is the most important characteristic of those successive waves. It is not their professional qualifications but their determination to get here that matters most. Remarkably, refugees, whether they had walked at midnight into Austria, or came north to protest a war, or packed themselves into dangerous boats in the South China Sea, or struggled here from Syria, seem to be as successful in Canada as conventional immigrants. That is because in every case the act of migration is that of a highly self-selected minority. Getting to Canada is neither procedurally or geographically easy. It is much harder than getting to the US or Europe. It requires determination, persistence and risk-taking, attributes ultimately far more important for success than paper qualifications. Immigrants are the entrepreneurs of life, unified by one clear objective: to do better here. If you cannot, why the hell did you come—that is every immigrant's midnight question and day-time motivation.

This is true, to some extent, of immigration to any city, but Toronto's unique advantage is that in the sheer number, that immigrant voice has become the city's dominant note. That is why, uniquely among global cities, immigration is welcomed. All those accidents of other people's history are what has made Toronto. Along, perhaps, with the consistent placidity of its native-born citizens. Peace, order and good government, minding your own business. There's something in the city's DNA that seems to have made immigrant acceptance easier, the flip-side of the city's relentless parochialism. Toronto has created home better than any city in the world, while simultaneously, and accidentally, jet-fueling its economic machine.

* * *

The Toronto urban region is thus growing faster than any other city in Canada, the U.S. or Europe. This megacity sits at the center of a rapidly filling cluster of connected regional centers including Hamilton, Kitchener-Waterloo, Oshawa and Barrie. A very big urban place is emerging. How big depends on who is counting. Statistics Canada, with characteristic Canadian modesty, puts the population of the region at 6.5 million. If we use the statistical methodology of the U.S. Census Bureau, we would be close to 13 million, making Toronto the third largest urban region after New York and Los Angeles, and at current rates of growth it will pass Los Angeles by mid-century. Interestingly, it is the only conurbation in the middle of the continent that is growing significantly, as the other great central cities are either shrinking, like St. Louis, or about to shrink, like Chicago.

Toronto's growth is why the second of Richard Florida's ideas is so important. Spikiness. The urban world is becoming spiky. Florida has produced a fascinating series of images of global spikiness. If you plot on the globe the distribution of PhDs, or new patent registrations, or start-up companies, or high-tech hiring, what you observe is how remarkably concentrated such activities are in just a few cities in a few countries on the planet. If you review the analysis of global financial centers prepared each quarter by the City of London, it is striking how only a dozen or so cities have any significant standing in what is, for better or worse, the core business activity of the global city. Once significant, independent financial service cities like Liverpool, Lyon and Hartford, Connecticut have lost their standings. In previous industrial eras, innovation might have been located close to coal or minerals or manufacturing facilities or port complexes; now essentially it is brains-located. Florida and his team are now decoding the critical determinants of these locations, attempting to isolate the DNA of the successful modern city.

There seem to be only a few key macro-determinants of global city success. First, size does matter. Big and bigger cities are the home of the new economy. Across the world, high-tech jobs are concentrated in a few large urban regions, financial services in even fewer. In the United States, half of all tech jobs are found in the Boston-to-Washington corridor and around San Francisco. The same spikiness is true for London and Shanghai. It is in these places that the ecology of high-tech culture has taken root, places with universities, venture capital, huge pools of specialized labor and talent and a highly connected airport.

The operational geography of these global cities is fascinating. Its higher-order financial services, business and high-tech innovations and trade functions demand connections to as many comparable world cities as possible, while at the same time its day-to-day operating success requires tight person-to-person contact. The need for close community in the context of global connectivity is what drives a large part of the spikiness. Fewer and fewer cities are getting better and better air linkages to more destinations, making airports a fundamental component of urban infrastructure. Travelling to Hong Kong, Singapore or Shanghai is to be dazzled by their understanding of that critical airport-city relationship. Business districts and trade and exhibition functions spring up right around them, connected to the city center by premium transit. Several European airports have recreated that chemistry—Amsterdam's Schiphol, Frankfurt Airport and Manchester Airport are all developing as critical elements of their city's competitiveness. In every global city, the area around the airport is the second largest employment cluster after the city center. And the reverse can also happen. Once significant U.S. airports like those in St. Louis, Philadelphia, Boston, Denver and perhaps even Chicago seem to be losing their international connectivity as a few key hubs like JFK, LAX and Toronto Pearson become the international entry points for the continent, re-enforcing their city's economic performance. Toronto Pearson is now the fastest growing and the fifth best internationally connected airport in the developed world, and currently the second international gateway to North America after JFK, which it could surpass in the next dozen years. All of this thanks to the mobility of the city's diverse diasporas, to the smarts of Air Canada and to what is probably the most effectively managed unit of the city's infrastructure, the Greater Toronto Airports Authority. It is in such obscure statistics that the emergence of Toronto is explained.

After airports, the second key determinant of a successful global city machine is advanced education. Remember the advice from the redoubtable Dr. Cheong in Singapore. Cities run on brains. Competition for standing in university rankings has become an aggressive part of any university's governance culture, and those seeking to maintain their funding and their ability to attract talent have no choice but to compete. The universities of Hong Kong and Singapore understand this. They continue their marches up the rankings, steadily edging out their Western competitors. When mainland China begins along that road in earnest, as it is just starting to do, there will be consequences for the West in terms of attracting and keeping their best academics. The University of Toronto, the once self-contented sleepy hollow at which I was a grad student forty years ago, now regularly ranks in the top twenty of world universities. A series of remarkable university presidents, notably Rob Prichard and Meric Gertler, have forced that institution into the world. Why are universities so important to the modern city? Because that is where the brains are. Florida's spiky world maps of innovation demonstrate the gravitational pull of great universities—they may not always be in the center of the urban region, but they are always within an hour's reach of the higher-order talent pool, the business opportunities, the international connectivity and the lifestyle that the metropolis provides.

I was riding my bike through the University of Toronto campus one sunny autumn Sunday morning. Located in the heart of the city on an urban super block, the tree-filled, gothic-collegiate campus has a quiet calm, resembling almost a Vatican City in scale and feel. It was frosh week and a parade of undergraduates in purple T-shirts and hard-hats snaked in front of me, blocking my way. It was the year's engineering entry class. By rough count it was two-thirds female, and the white-guy quotient was about 15 per cent, making for a happy collision of immigration, gender equality and higher education. The future of the city looked assured.

The third core driver of the contemporary global city is financial services. Everybody hates banks for their willful and still unaccounted for wrecking of the world economy a decade ago, for their excessive salaries, for their self-serving mystification of business practice and the way they siphon off talent from more productive activities. Nonetheless, in each of the top dozen world cities in which they are the key industry, and in most of the countries in which those cities are located, they are disproportionate generators of tax revenues. So be careful what you hate. In Toronto, the five national banks and the network of linked service providers generate 8 per cent of the city's property tax revenues. A city without a thriving financial services sector will have a hard time making ends meet. Toronto's rise to being one of the top eight world financial centers identified by the City of London's Global Financial Index has been recent, and it was confirmed by its remarkable stability through the 2008 financial crash. The bred-in-the-bone Scots/Irish Presbyterian caution of Canada's financial regulators and banking community, magically transmitted down the generations, had restrained it from some of the financial madness of its U.S. and European counterparts.

To a greater extent than any other economic activity, the banks, fund managers, insurance companies and other financial service providers represent a dense, extensive employment cluster, supporting key professional services such as law, accounting, management consulting, the increasingly important activity of fintech, not to mention real estate development. This, in turn, supports a myriad of printing, advertising, public relations, brokerage and design businesses, which then fuel the restaurants, hotels, theaters, nightlife, bars, specialty retail, delivery, media and cultural life of the city. Like it or not, the economy of the global city is top down. That broad multiplier effect of financial services creates the favorable conditions for smaller business creation, and lets those businesses take advantage of the global infrastructure the banks have created, reinforcing the spike.

* * *

Our firm, Urban Strategies, has a staff of around seventy people, tiny by the standards of our global competitors, yet we are able to compete for and service projects around the world. Why? Because we have an airport that connects us to everywhere, because we have a set of universities that provide superb new staff, because the banks and pension funds have spawned global development and investment companies to provide a solid business platform. We can only do business in a spiky city. And, of course, Toronto is a safe, easy, interesting place to live and raise a family, without which we could not hire the people we need from all over the world. That quality of urban life is the fourth determinant of city success, because livability attracts human capital, the mobile creative class that fuels the machine of the modern economy. Members of the creative class can work where they please. They will live where they can find a home.

Quality of life is an elusive measure. Toronto compares itself longingly to cities endowed by better geography, by those more greatly enriched by history. I have sat through endless self-satisfied lectures from Barcelona, Stockholm and Copenhagen recounting their perfections. Life is easier if you are a blessed with a pretty face and wealthy parentage. Spare me their smugness. Toronto, the plain child of world cities, was built too late and too quickly, and it has had to work harder. Again, true to its low church roots, it has succeeded through virtue, its unique brand of civic virtue.

I sit on the Governor's Council of the Toronto Public Library Board, which is my kind of committee because it never meets, except for drinks, and certainly does not govern anything. But it does provide me an insight into one of the most quietly impressive of Toronto's public institutions. As we have seen in London and New York, public libraries are in significant decline in most Western cities, unable to defend themselves against budget cuts, trivialized as museums for books, and condemned for being unresponsive to the changing behavior and technological preferences of their patrons. Library use, attendance and services are plummeting. Toronto is an absolute exception to the rule. Patronage is the highest of any municipal library system in the world, even in comparison to jurisdictions several times its size, receiving on average 70,000 visits a day. Far from closing buildings, the library board just opened its 100th branch in the north-eastern suburbs. The key to its success? Customizing services for the local community and becoming its useful, free, aspirational hub. It starts from the beginning: a new immigrant to Toronto receives a free library card upon arrival in Canada. At the library, he or she will find someone who speaks the same language, and back-home newspapers and books are on the shelves. Libraries are fully wired, offering internet access for free, positioning themselves as gateways to information about the wider, often confusing and daunting city in which they have just arrived. How do I get a driver's license, how do I register my kids in school, how do I get them immunization certificates, where do I go if I am facing eviction? The library staff can help. Preschool programs, homework clubs, language classes, reading circles, access to a printer—even a 3-D printer—or a digital music studio. Ultimately, the library is about citizenship, part of the alchemy of transition from reliance on ethnicity to connection to the broader community.

I recently took a skeptical European urbanist around Toronto. He found little to his taste. All was ugliness, congestion and sprawl. His perfect little German town, with a population just slightly larger than the annual population increases of Toronto, did everything better. I told him the story of the library system, which he silently doubted. As we were leaving the main branch he strode up to the fellow staffing the welcome desk and demanded: "How many languages do you speak?" The young man, of indiscernible, Toronto-blend ethnicity, answered almost apologetically, "About twenty, twenty-five." And clearly thinking this was insufficient, he pointed to the phone: "But I can get another fifty on the help line." The European retreated.

So the library system is the best in the world. The public school system is strong and generally scores high on the international PISA rankings, which means that both aspirational locals and middle-class talent moving to the city can send their kids to a free educational system without worry or embarrassment. There are shockingly few world cities, particularly in the English-speaking world, in which that is still true. The universities and a highly effective college system are publicly funded with remarkably low tuition fees, providing a readily accessible entry to the upper end of the economy. On top of this is Canada's universal access health care system, clearly less effective and efficient than the best in the world, but without a doubt better than that of the U.S., which for most is the important comparison.

Toronto, and Canada, provide public services that range between good and excellent. Neighborhoods have generally low rates of crime. There is no permanent, disaffected underclass of any size, unlike in so many Western cities. Peace, order and good government and what might be described as a commonwealth political sensibility have produced a culture and a chemistry that allow Toronto to excel at what is any city's most important task, the productive use of immigrant talent. Yes, there are significant challenges—in settlement, in accreditation, in affordable housing and in reconciling with the Indigenous population. Yes, it seems that more recent waves of immigration are taking longer to reach parity with the host population. But none of that changes the fact of Toronto's success on this score. Its well-functioning institutions and intelligent immigration policy enable social mobility and the constant refreshing of an aspirational middle class. After one generation, immigrant families achieve a slightly higher standard of living than those native born. In the United States, by comparison, the American Dream has all but disappeared. Only 7.5 per cent of children from the lowest fifth of the income scale will make it to the top fifth in their lifetimes. In Canada, the percentage is nearly double, with 13.5 per cent making the transition from bottom to top, more even than the vaunted Europeans.

Which leads us to Richard Florida's latest seminal urban insight, the unavoidable rise of urban inequality. There seems to be something inherent to the kinds of businesses that fuel growth in successful cities that they differentially reward the few. Florida describes this as a "winner-takes-all economy." Just a few great cities are eclipsing all other smaller cities and the non-urban world, and within them, the wealthy few are pulling away from the mass of the urban population. Nonetheless, while this pattern of neighborhood income segregation is by no means absent in Toronto, in comparison with most global cities, and certainly with the top dozen, Toronto seems to have the lowest level of internal inequality. The "Gini coefficient" is the generally

accepted measure of the spread of incomes—lower coefficients meaning a more equal spread between the richest and the poorest, higher
coefficients meaning greater inequality. Toronto has a Gini coefficient
of 0.41, New York 0.6 and Singapore a whopping 0.7.

Many are rightly offended by the notion of relative poverty.
According to "Unequal City," a recent report from Social Planning
Toronto, 125,675 Toronto children live in poverty, clearly an unaccept-
able number. To say that the city is less unequal than any other global
city is to invite accusations of complacency, and in low-church Toronto
that is a very bad thing. That is not my view, however. The continued
effectiveness of its public education, health, library and recreational
programs is Toronto's singular contribution to the urban world. That,
combined with the entrepreneurial vigor of 125,000 motivated newcomers, reminds us, in the era of Brexit and Trump, that liberal markets
and social democracy are the best approaches to running a country
and its cities. Most places in the West have lost that plot. And if people are unhappy with some people earning too much money, that is
what the income tax act is for, as the Trudeau government is demonstrating with its new taxes on high-income earners. Both Toronto and
Ontario governments followed that federal lead by introducing higher
minimum wages.

If there is a legitimate charge of complacency, it lies elsewhere,
in believing that our serendipitous and accidental rise can continue
without more conscious management of the economic competitiveness
of the city, and without greater care for the fundamentals of the city
as machine. The greatest risk for an immigrant city is that those new
residents have no way of realizing their dreams. The greatest risk for a
city growing as fast as Toronto is to frustrate those aspirations.

Toronto has the weakest, least capable governance system of any
of the world's leading cities. We have seen the effectiveness of New
York and London mayors, to say nothing of Singapore's unique city-
state. Toronto's mayor, although elected at large, has one vote on city
council. The remaining twenty-five city councilors, representing local
wards, each have a vote. The mayor must select his or her executive committee from this pool of councilors, which results in far less

impressive deputy mayors than those we found in other world cities. In practice, the mayor is the only political figure at City Hall who worries about the whole city, as the electoral dynamic works against any councilor being anything but intensely local in his or her interests. Councilors get re-elected time and again by pandering to small circles of local activists whose numbers are sufficient to ensure victory given low voter turnouts. Councilors are old, 69 per cent male and 87 per cent white. More than half have served more than fifteen years. Few have any experience of the world outside the council chamber. This may be fine for a parish council, but it is no way to run a great city. Ontario Premier Doug Ford's recent reductions to the size of council will, perhaps intentionally, have little impact on that structural inadequacy. Toronto is in deep financial distress, and barely able to provide or maintain its transit system or foster a reliable supply of affordable housing, let alone make critical investments in facilities necessary to maintain the city's global competitiveness. It may be a global city, but its leadership retains the suspicious instincts of a village.

If the Toronto region, which, again, is scheduled to surpass Los Angeles in population within a generation, fails to upgrade its infrastructure, if it allows traffic congestion to snarl to a stop, if it ceases to adequately fund the bedrock community services on which the city's success has been established, if it is unable to provide affordable housing at the scale of the problem, there will be a heavy price to pay. The city will still be receiving 125,000 new immigrants a year and if they cannot find work, if they cannot become full citizens, Toronto's happy accident will have an unhappy ending.

* * *

The corner of Weston Road and Finch Avenue is the ugliest place in Toronto. Finch is a heavy traffic, four-lane arterial, with a badly striped, slightly terrifying center turn lane. Full of trucks moving at high speed on disintegrating asphalt. Huge hydro-electric pylons overhead point at the westerly approach paths for Pearson Airport, just as lumbering planes begin to put their undercarriage down. To the south are 1960s high-rise apartment towers, randomly dropped into a landscape of bungalows. To the north are a warren of lock-up industrial units and broken junk land. Noisy, dusty, harsh. Even the Humber River has been frightened into a culvert. It is the kind of landscape all good urbanists hate, a complete surrender to cars and trucks, the city willfully turning its face from the street into a mess of low-rise shopping plazas. Concrete and asphalt everywhere. Random signage, no street trees or softness, successive generations of battered bus shelters and leaning light standards. Everything is broken and in need of repair. But quiet your dismissive mind and look more carefully. It is a world as rich in life as any wetland. What can we see?

In the half-kilometer stretch of Finch Avenue immediately west of Weston Road are five strip malls, each separated from the street by rows of parking, each a random mess of cheap low-rise buildings. They house thirty-six restaurants and food stores and about one hundred additional businesses. The thin sidewalks and random parking lots are full of people. Families, couples, groups of girls and guys, all shopping, hanging out, going to eat, talking. Everyone in the world is represented here except for white folk. No creative class coffee shops selling over-priced lattes. The restaurants, as far as I can tell from signage, represent about ten primary ethnic cuisines, eleven if you add in the Burger King and McDonald's stranded in the gas stations to the north, and many are idiosyncratic ethnic combinations. These ugly strip malls have the broadest range of food offering anywhere in a metropolis already known for its food variety. A Vietnamese place is selling the "world's best fish stew." There is a small Guyanese/Somalian/Jamaican food store advertising oxtail, goat, cow's feet, duck, drake and rooster. The Long Hui Supermarket has an enormous selection of crabs and snails. Indian and South American stores look relatively bland by comparison. And lots of ads for jobs. "Jobs, Jobs, Jobs," yell the signs. Minimum wage no doubt, but jobs.

Food preparation is Toronto's biggest private employment sector. The unique combination of the new city's diversity and the old city's reliable quality and standards enforcement have created North America's second largest food industry cluster after Chicago. In addition to the restaurants, there are hundreds of little businesses in this unprepossessing industrial zone, all different links on the food manufacturing chain. The location close to the airport helps. The bellies of the aircraft overhead are full of Italian-style cheeses and Punjabi roti, South Asian samosa and aphrodisiac sea cucumber, processed and packaged in these unprepossessing sheds and destined for the world.

The industrial lanes on the north side of Finch reveal a similarly rich ugliness. A sprawling 1960s small-unit industrial estate stretches north beside the rail tracks. Auto repair, tire stores, upholstery. Ominous barred windows and padlocked doors. Junked cars all around waiting for work. It is amazing how much business activity cars can generate. Then, suddenly, from a door I had not noticed behind an auto body shop, a multitude of magnificently dressed women explodes into the lane, laughing and shouting in long, white embroidered gowns and glorious headdresses. The Ethiopian Baptist Church. I look more carefully between the metal bashing sheds and the food processing companies. Small doors reveal a Hindu Temple and the El Nuevo Renacer, the Iglesia Cristo Viene, and a slightly larger place, the Pentecostal Faith Worship Centre. In this barren concrete ground, higher aspirations find their niche and their solace.

Back on the main street, it is suddenly impossible to miss the scale, intensity and diversity of the religious ecology of the district, something I had never noticed before. I may have been startled by that explosion of life from the hidden Baptist church but other religious buildings are now impossible to miss. A huge Prayer Palace has arrived like a spaceship one block east. Across the road is the curving, soaring spire of the Ghanaian Church of Toronto, right beside the Good Shepherd Chaldean Cathedral. Further down the street to the west are the Toronto Thiruchendur Murugan Temple and the North York Sikh Temple. These are industrial-scale buildings, packed during services, their parking lots as busy as those of shopping malls. From my apartment in downtown Toronto I can see the spires of half a dozen huge churches, the squat, solid sandstone and brick of United, Baptist, Anglican and Catholic parishes, all the religious *pentimento* of earlier waves of immigration. There is a vast onion-domed Ukrainian

Orthodox church a bit further west, peeking over the park. They are now all empty. Religion has moved on and out to where today's immigrants live. To the people who need it now. A Statistics Canada census tract perfectly captures the neighborhood. Two-thirds immigrant, over 90 per cent below average income, 93 per cent visible minority. The city initially designated this area as a "Priority Neighbourhood" but, ever worried about stigmatization, now calls it a "Priority Improvement Neighbourhood." The ring of similar areas around the increasingly wealthy central city are the frontlines of immigrant settlement, where every new Canadian looks first for housing, company and a job. It is rough and tough, with persistent crime issues in the many surrounding housing projects, although nothing to compare with the typical Western world city.

Habon Ali, a thirty-something urban planner, grew up here with her mom and brother and sisters. She is our guide now. We eat in Hakka No. 1, one of the Formica-table restaurants characteristic of the street, an unlikely Hakka/Indian fusion. It is good and very cheap. The less you pay in Toronto, the better you eat. We tour the main streets and the public housing projects that dot the neighborhood, not the big towers seen elsewhere in the city but mostly tight clusters of townhouses, a design mess of random buildings, alleys, parking spaces and left-over common spaces. "There are areas within the neighborhood that have always struggled with higher rates of violent crime and illegal activity. But there is also a strong sense of community, internal supports and eyes on the street," says Ali. As a kid, she rarely went downtown. This was home. The primary school was within walking distance, as was the big high school—Italian and Portuguese when her elder sister started but mostly Sri Lankan, Indian, Caribbean and Somali when Ali left. Right now it looks to be going Vietnamese. Each ethnic group kept to itself, as a tribe in the school. It was not until talent night or some similar event that everyone realized what an extraordinary place it was, and that as kids they all shared a love of music and stories of trouble and resistance from their homelands. We pass a prominent Canada Post street-corner mailbox and Ali jumps with excitement. "That was the key before- and after-school meeting place for me and my friends," she says.

Ali's mother arrived as a refugee from Somalia, through the United States. They got emergency housing and from there graduated to Toronto Community Housing. Yes, the neighborhood was sometimes sketchy. Yes, each new arrival group would be set upon by drugs and conflict. But by global city standards, it is still remarkably safe. It has functioning libraries and community recreation centers. The high school recognized and pushed talented kids. All four siblings in her family went to good public universities and have good jobs. One story, but the broader statistics suggest it is characteristic of the human ecology of Finch/Weston.

A successful city can and must do much to help newcomers. That infrastructure of good schools, welcoming libraries and recreation facilities is essential. Decent transit to jobs and opportunity is critical, and a new light-rail transit line is coming to Finch/Weston, hopefully to connect with the regional rail line further west. That new accessibility will transform the neighborhood. But I hope it does not wipe out the ugliness. Its very chaos is a critical feature of the district, part of its ugly beauty. Here one finds the first job with few questions asked and no skills required. Here are the cheap, flexible spaces for new start-up businesses, whether restaurants or auto wrecking—businesses that are an essential means of connecting new arrivals to the host society. Landlords care about collecting the rent, not about signage or cooking smells. Immigrants can find their own food, religion and language, even if it is in the midst of everyone else's foods, religions and languages. Put aside the embalmed beauty of Greenwich Village, Marylebone or Yorkville, and do not get distracted by the physical ugliness of Finch/Weston. This neighborhood is exactly what Jane Jacobs had in mind. The French have a word for it, *jolie laide*. An ugly beauty is born.

It is no accident that Toronto is the world capital of inter-ethnic marriage. Neighborhoods like Finch/Weston are human Petri dishes. They are also where Toronto's extraordinary music scene, led by Drake, The Weeknd and many more, is nurtured. Music is the great equalizer and the great mixer in a polyethnic city like Toronto, or "The 6ix," as it is becoming known, an appellation representing the six pre-amalgamation boroughs, or the 416 area code, or who knows what, and it does not matter anyway. The music springs from the malls and projects of North York, Scarborough and Etobicoke. Some of it in anger, yes, like such music from the same part of any world city, but as much in celebration and affection. It makes an interesting comparison with the music scene half a century earlier when Joni Mitchell and Neil Young found their voices in the city, downtown in Yorkville. They achieved international success and moved on to Los Angeles. Drake and The Weeknd can stay now. The city is finally spiky enough.

The relatively recent discipline of urban design, emerging as a response to an overly mechanistic culture of city planning, worries about the form and feel of the city but too often misses its function. The intersection of Finch and Weston, to any urban designer, looks like an urban patient on a sick bed, waiting for perfectly formed six-storey developments on either side of a street divided by a double row of trees. Waiting to look like a postcard of Paris. And it would look lovely no doubt. Bizarrely, a short fifty-meter stretch of development matching this description has already been built, with requisite paving stones and antique Victorian lampposts. The only problem is that all the stores are vacant. So, while I applaud the introduction of good rapid transit to Finch and Weston, I desperately hope they do not kill the rich, diverse, thriving human wetland that exists here. Please don't drain this swamp.

Heading back downtown, the sheer shabbiness of Toronto is unavoidable. Overhead a mass of wires hangs from bent wooden hydro poles. Is there a major city in the world that still provides its electricity through a hair-net of above road cables? The sheer number of poles and the tangle of wires are one of the most distinctive images of Toronto. I try to find some beauty in it but I cannot. Sometimes ugly is just ugly.

In the distance stands the CN Tower—it's remarkable how strong a presence it exerts even way north out here. That most enigmatic of structures. Is it beautiful, is it ugly? Or the apogee of ugly beauty. In each of the dozen places I've lived or worked in the city, I've had a view of it—even if one only seen when stretching out a window. Right now both my office and my apartment provide a full frontal and you can't avoid checking it out. It has a proportion problem, there's no doubt. While the logarithmic curve of the shaft seems just right, there's a nagging imbalance between the size, shape and spacing of the decks that I endlessly try to solve like a quadratic equation. And up close it's too easy to see all the misplaced transmission dishes, boxes and other randomly stapled-on junk, like warts on the face of a friend. And then there's the embarrassing hokeyness of the night-time lighting schemes. But it works out here, fifteen or more kilometers away; seeming wistful, slender, that most masculine of structures giving a feminine wave.

After the long drive from the suburbs, we are back in the old city, where I have always lived, and where everyone like me lives, with its familiar regular grid of tree-lined streets of two- and three-storey houses, all with their porches and gables. Comforting but also enclosing. Margaret Atwood's novel *Cat's Eye* captured that ambiguity perfectly:

> Underneath the flourish and the ostentation is the old city, street after street of thick red brick houses, with their front porch pillars like the off-white stems of toadstools and their watchful, calculating windows. Malicious, grudging, vindictive, implacable.

I have always thought this quote not only captures our unique aesthetic but stands as a good explanation for why Toronto has never been comfortable thinking of itself as a great city. But that was then. Something different is happening in the suburbs where the future of Toronto will be decided. We have been searching for beauty in all the wrong places. Let us remember the ugly beauty of Finch and Weston.

9

SYDNEY –
THE CHOCOLATE
TEAPOT

Another phone call. From David Pitchford, then the head of an Australian public development company called UrbanGrowth New South Wales, responsible for extensive landholdings in the largely abandoned old port of the city of Sydney.

"What exactly do you want to do on this site?" I asked.

"I don't know," he answered. "If I did I wouldn't be asking you. But I do know what I don't want. . . . I don't want a chocolate teapot." Followed by a wicked Australian grin I could see over the phone.

David Pitchford is one of the most experienced large-scale urban developers in the world. The initial summit of his career was his successful transformation of Melbourne, first as city manager and then as the person responsible for its acclaimed Commonwealth Games. He next built Dubai's over-the-top Palms development on islands off the city. Then he was hired by U.K. Prime Minister David Cameron to be his enforcer on a number of high-profile, high-budget projects, such as the 2012 London Olympics and the extension of the country's high-speed rail system. "David Cameron's ballbreaker" was how he was known in the raucous London press. He is a large man, tall, with the carriage of a former Australian Rules player. He comes from Tasmania, which must be a bit like coming from Newfoundland. The island isolation, sequestered by stormy seas, breeds larger than life personalities. He could hear the question mark that he had lit in my mind.

"I've spent my whole life getting chocolate teapots from some of the greatest architects in the world'," he explained. "Perfectly designed, perfectly finished architectural masterpieces. Great to look at. But put something hot in them and you've got an ugly mess. That's what I don't want."

Toronto and Sydney could not be more distinct, topographically or climatically. Toronto has a simple, binary relationship to Lake Ontario. It sits beside a long, straight lakeshore. Sydney has a gloriously complex internal and external coastline—it is literally embraced by the South Pacific—and on top of that, it has the postcard power of its Opera House, the Harbour Bridge, the bays and beaches.

Yet the first impression of Sydney, for me, is of utter familiarity. The feel on the street, in the downtown, on transit, in the parks, the restaurants and meeting rooms is intriguingly Toronto. It, too, is an immigrant city, a different mix but the same vibe. Sydneysiders and Torontonians are cousins, equally capable of creating a sense of home, although separated by a planet. Perhaps, again, it is that commonwealth sensibility. Both Canada and Australia have the phrase "peace, order and good government'" in their constitutions, a piece of colonial boilerplate no doubt but still expressive of their shared values, their friendly, open, easy presentation, their immigrant sympathy, their hint of deference and of being second-rate. The two cultures share what is known there as the cultural cringe, the fear that nothing they do is world class, the suspicion of anyone who tries to break out. Although to be completely accurate, Aussies are a lot louder.

Sydney also has the same opportunities and problems as Toronto. It is a merchant city, not a national capital. It is a big city in a vast, underpopulated country. Just as nine out of ten Canadians live within a hundred kilometers of the U.S. border with half a continent of rock, trees and ice to the north; the same proportion of Australians hug narrow strips along the south-east and western coasts of their huge, hot, mostly empty continent. There are similar cultural and political conflicts in both countries between their heartlands, dependent on extractive industries and agriculture and their increasingly urbanized fringes. Does the real Canada or Australia live in its wilds or its cities? The answer is obvious to Pitchford. He understands that the future of Australia will be played out in places like Sydney, and that there is no choice for a city but to compete globally. You can walk away from the fight if you like but you will be failing the future if you do. This perspective might be even more acute in Sydney than it is in Toronto. In any map of global cities, Sydney is the one in the far bottom right-hand corner, a long way from anywhere. It needs to wave a big flag to get anyone's attention. That is why it built the eye-catching Opera House and staged a very successful Olympics. The function of The Bays, as the old port on which we are working is to be renamed, is as the city's next advertisement for its future. It is to be the locus of the competitive machinery of Sydney's new economy. That is why Pitchford needs something more robust than a chocolate teapot.

The global city rankings reveal Sydney's weaknesses. It stands at the top of quality-of-life indices, alongside its Commonwealth cousins in Canada and New Zealand. But its economic heft is middling, its financial services sector is not in the top twenty and its best university, University of Sydney, sits in the low thirties. Comprehensive rankings tend to put Toronto and Sydney at about the same spot, just below the world's most significant cities, but they get there in different ways. Toronto has a more developed business sector. It is better connected to the rest of the world, and the University of Toronto ranks very high. Sydney is more middling but a hell of a nice place to live.

One significant constraint on Sydney's emergence as a global city is that, almost uniquely among developed nations, it has a serious urban competitor in the same country, just an hour away by plane. Melbourne is roughly the same size as Sydney with a growing economic and business center of its own. As a result, the relatively small urban heft of this vast country is split in two. If Montreal had not been the victim of Quebec's "civi-cidal" dance with separatism, it would be as big and powerful today as Melbourne—much to Toronto's and Canada's disadvantage.

Pitchford's objective is to use the large Bays site, deep in the back of the old harbor, way past the Opera House and behind the Sydney Harbour Bridge, as the place where the city's competitive urban edge can be advanced. He accepts the now universal playbook for waterfront planning I seem always to be drafting: environmentally sustainable, accessible, equitable, walkable, transit-friendly, with a welcoming, memorable, well-designed mix of office, retail and residential development of mixed heights, all in the setting of imaginatively designed open spaces. Pitchford, despite having the heft of Robert Moses, is ordering the full Jane Jacobs menu. But he wants it to be much more. He wants it to be the focus and driver of the city's future economy. He understands from his own experience that making all those delightful place-making attributes happen will first require initiatives big and important enough to change the geography of the city. As we saw in London, large-scale urban planning operates on old-fashioned physics. If you have a remote site you need a critical mass, a powerful, active destination, to draw people in and make it the place you want.

Right in the middle of The Bays is the White Bay Power Station, a huge, abandoned electricity-generating station that dates back to the nineteenth century, with many random additions. It is a glorious and iconic mash-up of steel girders, chimneys and brick detailing that dominate the waterfront, the kind of building every architect and preservationist gets excited about. But buildings of this scale fall victim to the London Battersea Power Station trap. You cannot preserve and refit a building so big and expensive unless you have a new use on the same scale. That magnificent, industrial-modern structure on the Thames designed by Gilbert Scott has been the subject of at least half a dozen failed schemes since its closing in 1983, and only now, with the benefit of patient Asian investment, has it found a second life as Apple's London headquarters, ringed by condominiums.

Pitchford wants to repurpose the power station and its surrounding lands as Australia's, and Asia's, leading high-tech innovation hub. What he had yet to work through, and what he wanted my help on, was how to make it happen. Sophocles famously noted that wars were won by men and money. Tactics, strategy, fine generals and noble intentions are all useless without those fundamentals. Just so with city building. Everything else is chocolate teapots. "Never start a project unless you know how to finish it," is Pitchford's mantra. The bigger and more idiosyncratic the project, the more difficult finishing becomes. You have to play the long and the short games simultaneously.

Sydney, like every great city, is an amalgam of villages and its idiosyncratic geography encourages localism. The innumerable inlets and bays of the harbor create tight little peninsulas defended by water. The endlessly serrated shoreline is a visual delight but also a haven for the narcissism of small differences. I hear it through the meeting chatter. "He's a Balmain boy, what do you expect." "Just another guy from Manly." The city of Sydney, situated at the heart of a metropolis of approximately six million people, has a population of just 300,000. Some forty other municipalities make up the rest of the urban region. Most, but not all of The Bays precinct is within Sydney, with other municipalities standing guardedly around.

To counterbalance Sydney's fragmentation, the state government of New South Wales and agencies like UrbanGrowth have been granted more power than their counterparts in other urban regions. This is essential for a project like The Bays. New York City and Toronto, by contrast, represent jurisdictions that are large enough and have sufficient political clout to balance but not displace the authority of New York State and the province of Ontario respectively, a recipe for stalemate rather than effective city management. David Pitchford's organization has its own extensive borrowing capability and it is able to call on both planning authority and compulsory purchasing power from New South Wales. If necessary, Pitchford can bypass the municipalities and go his own way. The state is way more powerful. It is not that simple, however.

The Lord Mayor of Sydney, the magnificently named Clover Moore, is not a person to be ignored. She is a local politician whose power base only increases when she clashes with the state. Winning office first in 2004 after a career in community organizing and now on her fourth term, Moore has fought heroically for the interests of Sydney against malign external powers. She is funny, imaginative and given to great hats. As the instigator of a number of substantial improvements to Sydney's urban environment, it is best to have her on board. But are there inherent conflicts between Sydney's global aspirations and its local territoriality?

* * *

Pitchford's first act is to host a massive international summit to which 400 local politicians, business leaders, cultural groups and academics are invited. Everyone with an interest in the redevelopment sits down with a travelling circus of ninety international urbanists for a two-day conversation exploring objectives for The Bays and looking at what the rest of the urban world is doing. I have been to a lot of these talk fests and Pitchford's is the most exuberant of its kind. Located in a sprawling, refurbished, former railway engine factory, all high girders and skylights, space is filled with temporary installations, presentations and meeting spaces. It is the only city planning conference I have attended with a walk-up oyster and raw bar. Cyclists offer ice cream to the milling crowd to mollify them for the lack of air conditioning. Local aboriginals perform a sweet grass ceremony. We are far from the dreary assembly rooms in second-rate hotels that are the cheese-paring standard for most planning events, and the medium is the message. It is difficult for the voices of localism to ignore the optimism, the examples of best practices from the rest of the world and the challenges to Sydney's global competitiveness.

Every urban regeneration agency has to deal with the fact that its reason for being is to bring transformational change to a local political environment that is suspicious of change, if not utterly opposed to it. The agency wants to invest in the machine of the city while the community cares primarily about home. To avoid diving straight into confrontations with local communities and their politicians, such agencies typically undertake extensive public outreach and engagement exercises, going far beyond the statutorily required public meeting to set up design workshops, steering committees and social media sites. The spirit of the times, with Jane Jacobs as its appropriate saint, is so firmly against top-down, expert-driven urban planning that a whole industry of public engagement has arisen to help the experts listen to the people.

Pitchford's conference is intended to initiate that process, but he starts by laying out ambitions that would never emerge from the local level. Fitting for a project of transformative scale and impact, he wants to redefine what community really means in the big city. It is not simply the local homeowners worried about traffic or the height of new buildings. Nor is community defined by environmentalists, heritage and architectural preservationists or aboriginal and equality activists, groups that typically fight to the bitter end for their particular interests. Nor is community a couple of developers who own some lots down the street or the café on the corner. On large-scale city building projects, community is all of them. Plus, two more constituencies that have far more at stake and are rarely heard from: the rest of the city whose livelihood depends on initiatives like these and the future generations who will be its beneficiaries.

Even the most energetic outreach program can only engage a fraction of all those affected by or with an interest in any major urban initiative. Most people never attend public meetings or read the outreach material or engage on social media. Waterfront Toronto, that city's fine development agency, conducted one of the most ambitious engagement processes ever. It held over 300 public meetings and outreach events in the past decade yet still made contact with less than 0.5 per cent of the city's population. I'm increasingly sympathetic to the Singaporean view that greater public involvement in major city building projects is profoundly undemocratic. It amplifies the voice of the haves rather than the have-nots. It places an unequal measure of power in the hands of those who turn up, usually older, affluent homeowners, or interest group adherents, without requiring of these same people any responsibility to address the hard choices of money, time and social equity that are fundamental to the expensive business of city building. These consultations also encourage a collateral irresponsibility among local politicians, who learn to use them to their advantage, letting the "community" make the decisions they were too craven to make themselves.

I calculated recently that I have been to about 500 public engagement sessions in my life as a city planner. I anticipate each with dread but usually end up enjoying them immensely. It is the activity that most distinguishes urban planning from all other professions. No aircraft captain or surgeon or accountant or dentist goes to a church basement to listen to *vox populi* tell them that they do not know what they are talking about and pinning better ideas to the boards on the wall. It is the closest thing to a Maoist cultural revolution as exists in contemporary professional life, with the experts banished to the corners of the city to take instruction from the people. As long as those meetings do not turn into an angry herd—and the skill of public engagement is to not let that happen—engaging directly with people you would never otherwise meet and finding a common language with them is one of the more enjoyable aspects of being a planner. And I never come away without having learned something or met someone interesting. As long as one remembers that it is just talk. The fundamental things apply.

* * *

Every city has its special place where you fall in love or salve a broken heart. In Toronto, it might be a walk through the ravines, or on the back seat of a streetcar as it takes a right angle turn. In London, it is the top deck, front seat of a red double-decker bus. In Sydney, it is on the ferries or at the beach.

In no other city are ferries so much a part of daily movement. Toronto has its island ferries and fine they are on a summer afternoon. London and New York have made huge strides towards making water transport a part of the daily commute but none compare to Sydney. The city has thirty-six wharves and a fleet of all kinds of large and small watercraft, each with its own unique design, engine song and motion. Double-bowed Manly ferries surge into Circular Quay. Motorized punts purr over to Balmain.

Every bit as fundamental to Sydney's culture are the beaches. Once I got to know the city, I moved from its downtown hotels to a place on Coogee Beach. Each morning I would stagger out of bed to watch the sunrise reveal that perfect neighborhood beach, a kilometer-wide crescent of sand that would already be packed with activity: the competitive teenage girl lifesaving teams, yoga practitioners, runners. Out beyond the surf line, you almost needed traffic signals to manage the flow of swimming groups churning back and forth across the bay. They nod and "g'day mate" as they stroke past. What bodies these beaches produce. The body beautiful from teenaged to centenarian: triangle shoulders and chest, straight spine, nipped waist. Sydney has to be one of the few places in the pale-skinned world where beach men give beach women serious competition.

It is a twenty-minute bus ride from the beach into town. The residential architecture along the way is a pleasant surprise, an array of low-rise neighborhoods running up and down the steep hillsides of the city. Small, one-storey and two-storey Victorian houses with filigree wrought-iron verandahs and red tile roofs, steep-pitched for subtropical downpours. The neighborhoods are linked by continuous main streets lined with two-storey buildings, sidewalk-shading canopies obscuring their frivolously decorated upper floors. As in Toronto, there is mile after mile of immigrant shops: the starter food, restaurant, nail salon and travel businesses that are the entryways to entrepreneurship. Strips like these are the wetlands of the urban economic ecosystem. Ugly, unkempt and essential.

Closer to the center, from a sidewalk or an upper window, you can catch a glimpse of the bay and a piece of the over-lapping white shells that make up the Opera House roof and, beyond, the curve of the Harbour Bridge. In these streets, the transformative urban newcomer groups are increasingly evident, the twenty- and thirty-something workers of the new economy. Sidewalk cafés, minimalist meeting places, retro furniture and housewares shops, alternative art galleries, restaurants and bars. Sydney's inner city neighborhoods are rapidly gentrifying, prompting a terrifying surge in housing prices. Lisa Pryor captured the feeling in the *New York Times*: "These urban villages, once diverse melting pots, became shiny, wealthy, and inward looking. The big ideas became small and hard as sparkling diamonds."

I think she had Balmain particularly in mind. In its earlier life, Balmain was notorious as Sydney's communist neighborhood, with an Irish Catholic working-class culture that gave the city much of its swagger. Today it is gentrifying at a phenomenal pace. It is the most perfect of districts, just a short ferry across the harbor from the center, with a gloriously active, pedestrian-friendly main street thrust out along a peninsula overlooking The Bays. Housing prices are skyrocketing. In a few years, as the adjacent neighborhoods are taken over by a new urban class with more money in its pockets, the restaurant and store offerings will move steadily up-market. One Sydney observer posits a "goat cheese line" delineating the moving urban boundary within which the smart set resides and goat cheese is served with everything. Sydney, San Francisco, Vancouver and Hong Kong—the four bayside cities with the highest housing prices in the world—are each being scrubbed clean by wealth and it is not at all clear what, if anything, a city can do about it. In an interesting innovation, both the British Columbia and Ontario governments have recently slapped fierce taxes on foreign buyers of Vancouver and Toronto real estate. The jury is out on their long-term effectiveness but for now they seem to have gently burst the housing bubble. Hong Kong has taken much the same approach and now there is talk that Sydney might follow. Its housing prices are close to being the most expensive in the world, way out of whack with its real economic position.

Among Sydney's many geological blessings is the fact that it sits on a honey-striped, stream-bedded sandstone that cuts clean and carves like a dream. The Victorian houses are built out of it. All you need is a saw and you can cut yourself a house. Hawkesbury Sandstone, known as Yellow block, is the city's ever-present architectural base note, amplified in the center with a spirited collection of Georgian banks, public buildings and shopping emporia, each carved to within an inch of its life. Against the tight grid, the stone gates and walls, domes and dormers, are the flowering shrubs: bougainvillea, ailanthus, flashes of color against the deep, fleshy sub-tropical green.

Life is lived outdoors in Sydney, creating streets of endless café tables. What a price we pay for winter in Toronto. There is a frivolity to Sydney's neighborhoods that could never withstand a serious ice storm. Frost heave, freeze/thaw cracking, differential expansion, to say nothing of snowplows, would devastate the streetscapes of Sydney and Singapore. Instead of year-round green and year-round *al fresco* cafés, Toronto has an eternal scruffiness. Winter has a lot to answer for.

At the end of the bus ride I'm convinced Sydney is the best place in the world to live. It is Vancouver with a decent climate. Barcelona with an economy. Hong Kong with some gentle relief. San Francisco without fog and trust-fund brats. It is just as well that it is on the other side of the world, only accessible by a grueling flight, or housing prices would be still more ridiculous.

* * *

The strategy for the regeneration of The Bays rests on the successful execution of two projects. One, the re-creation of Sydney's famed Fish Market into a full-blown tourism destination, seems well underway, Pitchford having herded the unruly bunch of fishers and fish wholesalers into accepting the idea of moving to new premises next door. Sydney is already the largest fish market in the southern hemisphere. Three million tourists visit it each year. Pitchford wants to double that number, making the market one of the city's top attractions. He will keep the wholesale function of the market, preserve the wharves for the local fishing fleet and charter vessels and replace the rest of the market's tired, run-down facilities with dramatically new viewing areas, indoor and outdoor restaurants. Opening is scheduled for 2022.

His second, more important project, and the one on which he sees the overall Bays strategy succeeding or failing is the creation of one of the world's leading innovation districts in and around the White Bay Power Station.

Innovation districts have become the holy grail of the contemporary global city, a critical new driver in the modern urban machine, a place that, to quote the enthusiastic prose of the Brookings Institution, forges "a synergistic relationship between people, firms and place (the physical geography of a district)" and "facilitates idea generation and accelerates commercialization." Each generation of economic activity has its distinctive physical environments that become the crucibles of new economic activity, places where the chemistry of brains, money and risk come together in a new way. The coffee houses of eighteenth-century London gave rise to limited liability companies. The cotton, coal and grain exchange floors of the nineteenth-century U.S. and U.K. business worlds were where the price of a good could be continuously determined in real time. The digitization of business might have been thought to eliminate the need for close personal contact but the rapid creation of innovation districts in cities around the world suggests otherwise, a pleasant reminder that people, in all their glorious and awkward individuality, are always the most important element in a city's success. People and the spaces in which they work.

What distinguishes all the successful contemporary innovation districts seems to be the integral role of their physical environment, as if the atoms of innovation can only be combined into a competitive molecule within the right form of buildings, a creative blend of indoor and outdoor spaces, fluid patterns of movement and a rich mix of activities, perhaps even a mix of old and new. Jane Jacobs famously observed that new ideas always emerge from old buildings. In her analysis, this was largely because new businesses cannot afford new space. But there does seem to be something almost deterministic in the productivity of the converted brick and beam warehouses or extensively glazed, exposed steel-frame structures that now characteristically house new innovation activity.

A fierce and important debate is underway in major cities about the role of the big tech companies in catalyzing a city's innovation activity. It is hard to overstate the market position held by the four big tech giants: Amazon, Google, Facebook, Microsoft. Their collective U.S. operations employ close to a third of the nation's recent math and computer science grads. In a very real sense these companies have become the equivalent of automobile plants in the 1960s, the core economic activity of a region. Their impact on cities is none the less profound, not only their job-creating multiplier effect but their accelerative impact on a city's housing markets and the heightening sense of income inequality. *The London Times* recently reported that the 3,280 Google staff in the U.K., mostly in London, were paid an average of £200,000. Great people to have in your city, but can you afford them?

I had a minor role in helping to prepare Toronto's response to Amazon's recent contest to identify a host city for its second headquarters complex, a facility that would ultimately house 50,000 employees, earning an average of $100,000, seemingly modest by Google's standard. This competition was fascinating—as horse race, as a defining moment for the contemporary city machine and for raising all the issues that urban spikiness brings. Amazon's requirements for its future HQ city brought together in one short list all the features we have seen on our city tour. First-rank university brain power, air connectivity, a functioning transit system and a sense of cultural achievement and community ambition. What was not clear was whether they were also looking for substantial tax breaks and/or financial incentives. To a greater or lesser degree, most of the twenty cities they short-listed had moved in that direction. Toronto, to its credit, did not. There is something profoundly immoral, a Faustian bargain, about trying to bribe one of the world's largest companies, led by the richest man in the world, to locate in your city. Toronto instead committed to a step change in the number of STEM (science, technology, engineering and math) grads in the province, demonstrating a sophisticated understanding of the operational economics of the tech industry, to whom a one-time tax credit or cash infusion, effectively a municipal bribe, is almost irrelevant. Amazon's ultimate choice to split its new headquarters between Long Island City and suburban Washington, D.C. was enabled by very significant inducements. Not city building's finest hour.

Each innovation district has its own unique make-up with a consistent set of components. In the South Union district of Seattle, a private developer and the city combined to transform a dilapidated low-rise warehouse district into a hub of housing, transit, global technology and life science firms. The real goal of that project, however, was to convince Amazon to locate its first 1.6-million-square-foot headquarters there. It has had a dramatically beneficial effect on the area, although perhaps no one could have anticipated quite how success-ful it would be, and quite what dominance Amazon would establish in the city. Our London tour identified an urban arc rather than a district of innovation, stretching from King's Cross to the new busi-ness hubs of Clerkenwell, on through the old warehouse districts of Hackney and Shoreditch to Tech City, home to a major Google pres-ence at Silicon Roundabout, then further east to the Here East project in Queen Elizabeth Park. In Toronto, the Medical and Related Sciences Discovery District (MaRS), is a two-million-square-foot, state-of-the-art innovation complex situated between the University of Toronto, the provincial government buildings, and a cluster of large hospitals, the trifecta of forces seemingly necessary to generate commercial biotech activity.

Each of these unique physical environments and organizational settings combines the essential DNA of highly trained researchers, university and government funding and support, an entrepreneurial ethos and a casual, mingled work environment in a highly urban-ized location. There is a story that best captures that spirit. MaRS is a complex that combines renovated former hospital buildings, a retail and food concourse and meeting rooms along with high-tech wet labs, research space and offices for lawyers, venture capitalists, accountants, intellectual property specialists and the like. At the outset, none of the separate occupants of the complex ever met. They kept to their own spaces, passing without interaction in the soaring sky-lit pathways between old and new buildings—until the MaRS organization started Friday evening socials and an ice hockey league. The curve of patent production immediately started to trend upwards.

The one example of an innovation district that fascinates David Pitchford and everyone in the business of urban planning is Cornell Tech on New York's Roosevelt Island. Could Sydney replicate that on the former power station site? Great cities are like jackdaws, fasci-nated by the newest flashy thing in the nests of their competitors: the Bilbao Guggenheim; the Tate Modern; Stockholm's new enviro-max communities; Crossrail, Curitiba's bargain-basement but effective tran-sit system; Sao Paulo's gondolas. Cornell Tech, right now, is the "it" project for almost every city that has its head up and David Pitchford was sure to involve its progenitors in The Bays.

To catch a fish you have to bait the hook. To land a whale something more is required. Pitchford issued his own request for proposals (RFP) for tech development ideas for the White Bay Power Station. The response was unsatisfactory. Thirteen entries, mostly from conventional developers, who proposed masses of unexciting high-rise residential buildings, never mind that the site was purposed as an innovation district. As a former developer, Pitchford has a healthy disdain for his industry, and it was confirmed by this response. Like a lot of city builders, it does not take much to trigger his rants against mediocrity. But the RFP did flush out one key party: Google. Its submission, part of a wider bid from the mega-developer Lend Lease, was a one-sentence response effectively saying, "We are interested."

Pitchford cancelled the RFP process, happily said goodbye to the developers and got permission from the dauntingly named New South Wales Independent Commission Against Corruption to commence exclusive negotiations with Google. Exclusive negotiations and sole source bids are frequently the ways in which civil servants end up in the newspapers or in jail. You need nerves of steel to recommend such a course. Pitchford pushed ahead. The proposal as it developed involved Google occupying the entirety of the old power station, transforming it into its Asian/Australian headquarters. It would employ 5,000 people in over a million square feet of space. Surrounding Google, Pitchford had corralled satellite campuses of the city's major universities, as well as campuses of several overseas universities. In the next ring out would be a mass of high- and low-tech research, start-ups and incubators.

For almost a year, Pitchford's team hammered out the details. Google has the awesome power that comes with being a global monopoly and it bargained hard, but much of what it wanted were things Pitchford also wanted. For instance, the company insisted the state government commit to a phased series of transit improvements, starting with rapid bus transit, moving to light rail and ultimately adding heavy rail to the west and to the planned new airport. As the project took shape, it became clear that it had the potential to establish Sydney as the new global leader in wrestling the tech sector to mutually beneficial urban outcomes. And the critical mass and leverage of Pitchford's strategic location would enable all those community-loved, smaller, urban-friendly waterfront initiatives to actually happen.

* * *

I also go swimming in the evening when Sydney's glorious beaches are more relaxed, without the morning's frenetic determination. There is no better way to end a working day. Heading back into Coogee afterwards, I walk down its neighborly main street, past a shade-tree-circled cricket pitch in the center of town. There is an abundance of great seafood restaurants. I check out *A Fish called Coogee,* a cash-only hole in the wall, part take-out, part eat-in. If you take one of the shared bench seats you can bring your own booze; a Tasmanian chardonnay from the wine store next door is recommended. Rock oysters, octopus, big and little shrimp, calamari and something tasty that I have never seen before with the unappealing name of "bugs." The local fish, barramundi, comes grilled or battered. The staff behind the counter have the cheerfully dismissive attitude characteristic of a good fish restaurant. They are busy shucking, so get out of the way. I am a happy man, resting with a glass of cold, dry white wine, relieved to hang out ahead of tomorrow's long flight to Shanghai on what I fear will be a fool's errand. An urban beachfront is as perfect as it gets. From my bench I can hear the waves. It is high tide tonight, so the waves are big, two meters or more, crashing against the rocks in a champagne of surf.

What did Sydney tell me? That making a successful city top down is more important than bottom up? That to think otherwise is chocolate tea-pot indulgence. That only massive projects are transformative enough to ensure that everything smaller will follow? That it takes a ball-breaker to build a city? Not entirely sure about that last one but I am warming to my subject.

Then I get a call. Pitchford. The state has balked. Google has walked. The transit commitment is too rich. With every Sydney politician screaming for funding for his or her pet local scheme, building the future is a bridge too far. Local consumption has beaten long-term investment, the curse of community-driven politics. The lead tenant has also generated animosity: "Why should Google get a special deal when they don't pay taxes anywhere anyway?" It is hard to argue that Google should not pay a lot more tax. It would be in the company's interest. Meanwhile, Sydney will have wait to modernize its machine. And Pitchford is out of a job.

Later in the trip, I receive two oddly coincident messages. One informs me that an Alphabet/Google subsidiary, Sidewalk Labs, has just won a competition to prepare an urban innovation plan for part of the Toronto waterfront. The other is about involvement in Toronto's Amazon HQ2 bid. There is no getting away from these guys. Global digital companies are now major forces in the modern city, and cities have not figured out how to deal with them.

10

SHANGHAI – CAPITAL OF THE FUTURE

Sydney to Shanghai is seven hours or more. I arrive late in the evening at Pudong Airport, feeling wiped. Pudong is another vast, modern, perfect piece of Asian infrastructure. I leave it on a perfect, super-fast mag levitation train that carries me at more than 300 kilometers per hour towards the city, where things rapidly go sour. The terminus is a nowhere-land concrete and glass shed with, to the uninitiated, no obvious exit to the city. I trail my luggage down endless corridors and through acres of asphalt looking for civilization. I know that I have made some newcomer's wrong turn but I cannot determine where. Tired and stupid, I flag down a random taxi. A bad move.

The opening scene in the movie *Lost in Translation* has the recently landed, jet-lagged Bill Murray character make a similar midnight entry into Tokyo, the taxi window reflecting the freeway, the ads, the traffic and his dead-eyed unknowing of this new place. I do not know where I am, what time of day it is, how much this taxi ride should cost, how the money really translates, where the hotel is and what the fastest way to get there might be. I am in the hands of a guy who speaks no English and I have no choice but to trust him. My trust in the driver is misplaced. He is unable to find the entrance to the hotel. I have had enough so he dumps me on a narrow street outside a camel milk shop. I am sure he seriously rips me off but I am unable to estimate the damage. I wheel my bag this way and that and eventually find reception. Once in my room, a wave of life-loathing sweeps over me. This is what I do for a living. A no-account consultant, a hunter-gatherer addicted to jet fuel.

I sleep, sort of, and awaken, gratefully, to a sweet sunny day. The trials and the doubts of the previous night have mercifully receded. The missed exits and the taxi driver are now just another war story. Thank you and good morning, Shanghai.

I had asked two of the city's natives in my office to advise me on people and places to see. They have assembled a veritable tour guide. A great advantage of working in so diverse a design office is that I can receive knowledgeable, practical creative work on almost any place in the world. The first tour recommended for me is close to the hotel. Just what I need.

Fuxing Park is in the French Concession at the center of the old city. It wears its French origins well. With its combination of formal *allées*, close-trimmed *ronds-points* and arbored paths one could easily be in Nantes or Tours or any other pleasantly bourgeois French provincial town. Except that here, at eight in the morning under the broad sweep of the plane trees, the locals are ballroom dancing. Mostly to old show tunes but sometimes to something Latin of the same era. It is largely couples, of all ages, with a few female pairs. Formal and decorous. Elbows high, leads firm. There is one fine man with a Gene Kelly smile, tall, slim, well suited, straight-backed and not much shy of eighty. Quite a few women line up for him. He is worth it.

Shaking off my jet lag, I note what else can be seen from the park bench. Further down are other groups of dancers, slow waltzing to classical Chinese music. Off in a corner are serious games of cards. Four or five sharp-eyed players at each table with a half dozen more looking intently over their shoulders. Cards are slammed on the table and money moves fast. Clearly this is how they earn a living. Further away, in front of a faux-grotto, a baton-wielding, barrel-chested conductor leads a small choir in traditional songs, pointing out the words on a well-used board.

On the *parterres* and lawns, there is more activity. No space goes to waste. The Chinese may not be crazy for team sports but they invent a remarkable array of exercise routines. Highly energetic kite flying, fluid games of court-less badminton, deft spool tossing, individual and group tai chi. Everything done with great concentration. In one pleasantly walled section of the park is a gloriously 1950s children's playground without an item of contemporary play equipment such as climbers, swings or slides. Here are bumper cars, a tiny electric railway, a carousel and noisy electronic games. The kids love it. And none of them are overweight. Unlike most formal French gardens there is next to no statuary. One major exception is at the top of the *allée* where Marx and Engels, huge in red granite, smile benignly over their progeny. If there is a proof of perfect delight in a city, surely this is it: to sit in an unknown park, in the early morning comfort of strangers and watch the city waltz.

Shanghai occupies a critical geopolitical position at the delta of the Yangtze River, the great route into China's interior, and for much of its history it has been the Chinese city most engaged with the rest of the world. It is always worth remembering that for 2,000 years China was the most populous and prosperous country on earth. It was only in the eighteenth and nineteenth centuries that European, American and Japanese powers challenged its supremacy. The logic of China's size and foundational geography is now vigorously reasserting itself. China's current leader, Xi Jinping, has in the delightful lexicon of Chinese planning introduced the notion of One Belt and One Road to characterize his country's newly declared geo-political economic strategy. The One Belt is the newly reconstituted Silk Road, which for much of its route inside China follows the Yangtze. One Belt is being re-invented as a high-speed rail route leading from Shanghai to the interior and on through Eurasia, as well as to Malaysia and Singapore. The One Road consists of the network of sea routes springing from the megacities running along the country's eastern maritime border, principally centered on Beijing, Shanghai and Hong Kong. Now, as through China's extraordinary history, the One Belt and the One Road intersect at Shanghai. The western terminus of the One Belt rail line is, wonderfully, in Barking; the irrepressible Darren Rodwell met the first train in 2017, hoping wistfully as he did so that he would have something to send back to China.

London and New York, the world's current leading cities, share Shanghai's foundational geographic logic. Their safe harbors are easily accessible to the world's trade, and their Thames and Hudson Rivers provide a ready route to a huge hinterland. Despite all the changes in transport modes and technology, geography will out, which is why Shanghai will be the capital city of the future. The world's center of economic gravity is steadily moving back to where it started.

Shanghai currently has a population of 24 million, almost equal to those two other global urban leaders combined, and it is projected to grow to between 35 and 45 million by 2050, with the surrounding Yangtze Delta region surging to about 200 million. This extraordinary rate of growth has been consistent since the 1980s when the population of the city was less than half of what it is today. What is remarkable about Shanghai, and why it is so significant an example of the planet's relentless urbanization, is that few if any cities have coped with such dramatic urban growth as effectively.

Shanghai's modern history starts after the Opium Wars in the early nineteenth century when Great Britain, in what still stands as one of the most disreputable acts in history, forced the declining Qing Dynasty to permit the British to trade the drug in the Middle Kingdom. Their entrée was followed by the other colonial powers, France, Japan and the U.S., who also extracted terms for permanent, quasi-autonomous national settlements on Chinese territory. These survived until the Second World War and, in the case of Hong Kong, right up until the end of the twentieth century. Anyone wishing to do business in China does well to acknowledge that Chinese memories of these matters are long.

The city grew rapidly as China's primary trading post and financial center, taking advantage of its strategic positioning. Shanghai's historic center was on the west bank of the Huangpu River where the tributary Suxhou Creek provided the protected berthing from the China Sea. A fine line of mid-nineteenth-century merchant buildings known as the Bund runs south of the creek, sharing an uncanny architectural similarity to the similarly located "three graces" buildings on the Liverpool riverfront. Behind them were the International Settlement and the French Concession.

The middle part of the twentieth century did not treat Shanghai well. Japanese aggression through the 1930s culminated in the invasion of 1941, which was followed by China's civil war. Stability eluded the city until the communist victory in 1949 and even then Mao's victorious government did not hold Shanghai in high regard, despite the fact the Chinese Communist Party had been founded in the city. His disastrous experiment with the Cultural Revolution, directed particularly against cities and the educated middle class, further weakened Shanghai and its inherent competitive advantage lay dormant until the 1980s.

The regeneration of the city dates from the death of Mao and the ascension to national power of Deng Xiaoping, who transformed China into the economic powerhouse it is today. It was Deng who set the economic table for Shanghai, allowing it to resume its urban primacy. As we noted in Singapore, he shared Lee Kuan Yew's origins in south China's remarkable Hakka Han ethnic community. They were close confidants in the building of an original, modern Chinese society, both economically and socially.

Planning for Shanghai's future started in earnest in the late 1980s, with a vision and an effectiveness unmatched in urban history. Haussmann's mid-nineteenth-century remake of Paris might come closest, but even that monumental and rapid urban transformation pales in comparison to the past thirty years in Shanghai. All Robert Moses' megalomaniac visions for New York would not even make the scorecard. Shanghai decided to completely retool its machine. Just one statistic: Shanghai's metro system, with its twelve lines, is now the most extensive in the world, yet its first line only opened in 1993. Four new lines are under construction and five existing lines are being extended. No city outside of China can compete with so comprehensive a transit expansion, and that is just one facet of the rebuild. Shanghai has provided one of the world's largest and most rapidly growing urban populations with a quality of life and a breadth of infrastructure unmatched by any other megalopolis. It has done so in less than three decades without benefit of the sort of Victorian urban inheritance enjoyed by Western cities.

* * *

It is time to get off the park bench and start my appointments. I head back to the hotel to change and find a confusion of messages in Chinglish waiting for me. Meetings have been cancelled or moved but details are imprecise. I spend a moment feeling absurd, a Canadian consultant from a city that has barely been able to build a kilometer of transit in the past three decades, a city that could fit several times into Shanghai, about to peddle his dubious planning wares to these masterful people. Eventually things get sorted out and I head downtown to meet with an architectural firm and its publicist about a high-tech project in one of Shanghai's suburban centers. The firm would like to partner with us. At least, I think they would. As in a lot of business meetings in China, language travels with a fluidity that leaves me feeling like a hick. When we speak English, it sounds more like some parallel language in which familiar words and phrases float free of their moorings. The key moves are discussed in Chinese, which my co-workers may or may not understand.

The meeting is over as fast as it began. We shake hands. Documents are to pass between us. Further ventures will be explored. I leave a little dazed. In the base of the office complex is the inevitable multi-floor retail plaza. Sitting with a post-meeting coffee, I can see all the high-end shops: Armani, Bally, Calvin Klein, Lanvin, Jimmy Choo, Hermes, Vertu, Berlutti, Dior, Max, Prada. A roster repeated throughout this city, throughout Asia, multiple times. All they seem to lack is paying customers. The stores are mostly full of well-turned-out younger women, their modest gazes suggesting more religious than retail behavior. The men who walk by have the hard eyes and self-confident body language you see in all great cities. They flick between back-slapping greetings and glances at their mobiles or Piaget wristwatches.

The office building and retail plaza are plugged directly into the metro station three levels below. All of the stations have the same generic layout. A platform level with the best-designed platforms, safety doors, and signage I have seen in any city. A generous inside-the-fare-zone mezzanine level above the platforms allows for easy interchange between lines and provides multiple exits directly to build-ings and the street system. It, too, is filled with shopping, although at a considerably reduced price point than the floors above, and the stores are filled with paying customers. Above the street and lobby level is the up-scale retail concourse where I am drinking coffee. Shanghai has laid its dozen transit lines roughly on a grid, spaced one-and-a-half to two kilometers apart, and at every intersection there is a station like this, overbuilt with offices and apartments. The perfect chessboard arrange-ment for intensifying the city, providing accessibility and structure, a plug-in circuit board for serious injections of urban density.

This basic city design is important. Shanghai is growing at the rate of 700,000 to 800,000 people per year. Toronto, the fastest growing urban region in Europe or North America, is growing by only 100,000 to 125,000 per year. London and New York are far slower. If current trends continue, one billion people will live in China's cities by 2025. In that short time, the country will add a new urban population greater than the current population of the United States. Those new citizens will be migrants from the Chinese hinterland, and the majority will be living in one of the country's twenty-three cities with a population greater than five million, of which eight will have populations of more than ten mil-lion. Shanghai will be the largest. There has never been urbanization of this scale in the history of the world. All of the world's great cities are struggling to cope with growth and, generally speaking, they have no clue how to provide a decent quality of urban life to newcomers in such numbers. Yet, in a highly imperfect profession, Shanghai provides perhaps the best example of mega-scale urban planning that works.

Shanghai stands apart from much of China's recent urban growth. The country's first decades of urbanization were not terribly successful.

Heavy doses of Robert Moses with Jane Jacobs nowhere to be seen. Relentless stretches of tower blocks, mindless erasures of historic districts, freeways everywhere. All of the worst aspects of American development in the 1960s, but on steroids. Cities looked like vast science fiction movie sets. To his credit, President Xi Jinping recently called a series of party congresses to re-invent the rules for Chinese urbanization, advancing a series of principles with a distinct familiarity: urban growth boundaries, denser street networks, mix of uses, transit primacy, healthy communities, energy efficiency, good urban design. Jane Jacobs had arrived. It is fascinating when, in the Middle Kingdom, sensitive city building becomes a national government priority. China now has a fairly sophisticated planning and municipal government system, one that borrows the antique parlance of the U.K. with its 2008 Town and Country Planning Act. It wrestles with the same issues of top/down and bottom/up, with boundary fights between boroughs and the big city, with the status of detailed plans and urban design, with managing rampaging developers and quieting angry neighbors. I feel right at home.

Shanghai has been the exception and the leader of urbanization in China because its growth has actually been based on plans, a series of which have been developed since the 1980s. The themes of the plans are familiar to anyone who reads their equivalents in the big cities of Europe and North America: transit-oriented development, green corridors, heritage preservation, economic development, sustainability. The language of Shanghai's plans, however, is uniquely expressive. The new 2040 Plan translates as "Guiding Opinions on Compiling the General Urban Plan for a New Round of Overall Redevelopment in Shanghai." Its intent is to make Shanghai "a global city glittering with charm and attraction." The Shanghai Metropolitan Plan calls for "One Dragon Head, Four Centers." This means that Shanghai will be the dragon head of the entire Yangtze River region, containing an international economic center, a financial center, a trade and logistics center, and "an international center of socialist modernization." This is all to be achieved by 2020. I love this language. What a relief from the leaden prose in the comparable documents in most other cities. What is also different about Shanghai's plans is that they work. The city, already twice as dense as New York and London, and four times as dense as Toronto, has put itself in position to achieve one of the most difficult feats for so dynamic a metropolis: to stop sprawling and accommodate all its millions of newcomers within the current city boundary. That is why the carefully conceived, remarkably extensive grid of transit lines is so important. It provides a robust, flexible structure to carry the population that is coming. Rates of car ownership are still very low, about one-sixth that of the U.S., so the challenge is to see if, in the face of rapidly rising incomes and expectations, China can skip a whole generation of auto-based urban development and create the world's largest post-car city. That would be a gift to the world. And Shanghai will need to do it. Air pollution, exacerbated by the city's marshy maritime location, has a tangible presence.

The city's planning success is largely attributable to doing the big things well. The cleverest move was to recognize the scale of impending growth and create a massive urban relief valve across the river from the Bund by developing Pudong, a completely new downtown district. Thirty years ago a largely agricultural and low-intensity industrial area, Pudong is today the very model of the planned business and financial city center, home to a succession of stunning high-rise office towers. There were two essential drivers behind the creation of Pudong. First, to clearly establish Shanghai as the country's premier business center, in a central location with the scale to accommodate really large, tall buildings. Second, to relieve the pressure for redevelopment of the city's heritage districts.

The high-rise office towers have mostly been designed by foreign architects, raising the frequent query as to whether the Chinese will ever have the creativity and imagination to service a more consumer-based, high-value-added economy. The Shanghai Tower should set that silly question to rest. The most recent of the office towers, designed by Chinese architect Jun Xia, consists of a simple oval shaft cloaked in an elegant sheath dress reminiscent of a 1930s' ball gown. It shares the striking beauty of New York and Chicago office towers built in the glory days.

The great advantage of the city's mid-twentieth-century time-out was that it largely avoided the most destructive modernist era of city planning in the 1960s. Not entirely though, as there was a period of massive inner-city expressway building and slum clearance followed by the construction of dense tower blocks. In fairness, it is hard to imagine how Shanghai could have accommodated such massive population growth without some demolition. And I have to admit a secret delight in one of the most obviously destructive projects from this era, the double-helix expressway ramp spiraling down from the Nanpu Bridge. It is the acme of kinetic urban delight.

The majority of the traditional city fabric has been left in place. The Bund buildings, the French Concession, several historic neighborhoods including the original walled city, and numerous individual historic buildings remain with strict orders for their preservation. As a result, central Shanghai has a feel almost European in many parts. The French, in particular, left not only fine parks but a robust street grid that has proved highly adaptable to the city's growth, lined with mature plane trees and high-walled cantonments. Stucco and verdigris walls, heavy gates leading to inner passages, all with that magic mix of obviousness and concealment characteristic of a Haussmann *arrondissement*. In behind the gates are dense, maze-like districts, the *lilongs* that retain the mystery and memory of the old Shanghai of movies and legend, when the city was alternately known as "The Paris of the East" or "The Whore of the Orient."

* * *

Without Pudong, without the chessboard of high-intensity transit stations, the pressure for redevelopment of the *lilongs* would have been irresistible. Restaurants and shops occupy every nook and cranny of the street edge. The alleys of *shikumen*, tight nineteenth-century workers housing, are packed with businesses. Most of these are tiny, barely five or ten square meters, and each has a dedicated owner determined to make a living. It is that manic entrepreneurial drive that is the dominant note of Shanghai. Twenty-four-million utterly determined business people cannot be denied, and thousands more arrive every day. Even the sidewalks are cluttered with commerce as trucks full of heavy cardboard boxes, containing who knows what, pull over to be unloaded onto bicycles and ubiquitous electric scooters. There are endless stores brimming with junk. I try to count the number of use-less objects in one such shop: barrels of neon flip-flops, boxes of toy barking dogs, trays of umbrella cocktail sticks, a wall of garish luggage tags, a pile of plastic mini-guitars, three drums full of selfie sticks, trays and trays of hideously colored scarves and sexless underwear. It is as if containers of cheap, nasty goods destined for export refused to leave China.

The meter of a city is revealed on its sidewalks and intersections. How fast people walk, how aggressively drivers push into traffic. I have to instantly learn the protocol for cutting across or in front of other people who are moving in or out of my path. Shanghai would reach the finals of a world cup for close combat street behavior. I cannot believe the narrow calls but clearly, given the absence of actual bodies in the street, there is a well-understood system of signals and eye language that allows these crowded people to slip past each other on the side-walks, in their cars, on their bikes, on their silent electric velos piled high with goods. It is a denser dance of human molecules than I have observed anywhere else. Watching this exquisite, multi-modal bike/ traffic/pedestrian ballet at a French Concession intersection I picture its polar opposite. The characteristic Canadian prairie town where even to hint with head, hand or shoulder that you would like to cross the street brings all traffic to an instant, courteous stop. Each city has its own visible and invisible street choreography. It is one of the hardest things to learn.

I am led on a tour around Pudong by a member of its city planning team, a Shanghai native but educated, like so many of the profes-sional class I meet, at a first-rate European university, in her case *Pont et Chaussées*, one of the French *grandes écoles* that has a surprising presence in Asia. Indeed, the French origins of Pudong go a long way to explain the district's planning successes and failures. In the 1990s, the city government ran a series of design competitions to determine the best layout for the new city district, involving many of the world's great architectural practices. To give the new district some overall coherence they turned to the Paris regional government for advice. The pattern of *rond-points* and *grand boulevards* that resulted do undoubtedly establish a greater urban order but much has been executed at so absurdly over-sized a scale that the environment at street level is unfriendly and charmless. Pudong demonstrates more clearly than any other new city district I know why large-scale city building has to be led by planners and not architects. Architects always get it wrong when they are given a problem that is too large. They treat a city district as if it were merely a bigger building, an abstract code of angles and intersections, rather than as an organic place that must be allowed to evolve into its optimal form.

Pudong is fixable, however, if only because the massive densities involved are generating enough human activity to take over even poorly designed spaces. A program of de-engineering is underway to reduce the amount of space devoted to automobiles. In the center, at Lujiazui, the city has given up on the street level entirely and created a huge, circular, above-grade walkway accessible by escalator and connecting to all surrounding buildings. It breaks every rule of contemporary city planning and is a great success, full of liveliness and an endless selfie opportunity.

My guide tells me of the difficulties for young, aspiring professionals who live in Shanghai, which sound much the same as those in every successful city. While office rents have been flat over the past decade, housing costs have increased three to four times. Residential property prices have exploded, forcing choices between desired but cramped city-center living and or a long commute from way out in the family-friendly suburbs. One bright note is that since the private sector replaced the state as the main housing supplier, units are becoming more numerous and more spacious. My guide has a boyfriend, she tells me, shyly, who lives in Canmore, Alberta. "Is it a nice place?" she asks. A snow-peaked Rockies postcard flashes through my mind. A greater contrast to Shanghai is hard to imagine. Then she tells me that the deadline for the competition I am chasing for the master planning of the Pudong Riverfront closed the week before my arrival. I feel I am dropping the ball left, right and center.

Like all great places, this vast city has no interest in my screw ups. I bounce off its disinterest, and take a long subway ride out to the suburbs, to the end of the line. I was intending to see the lovely lakeside city of Hangzhou, location of the 2016 G20 summit. You get to Hangzhou from the railway station at Hongqiao, which is also the terminus of the high-speed rail to Beijing. It is a multi-layered rail, bus and air terminal building of a scale and ambition quite unmatched by anything in Europe or North America. My attempts to buy a ticket are defeated by the queues, my lack of Chinese, my confusion regarding payments and schedules and my general lack of urban gumption, not to mention an unmistakable sense of panic. I was intimidated by the vast windowless building, the swirling crowds, the insignificance of my Canadianness despite my height and bulk. I got lost down on the lowest level and felt as if I was underwater, drowning. Desperate for contact with the outdoors, any outdoors, I swam up a series of limit-less escalators to catch a glimpse of sunshine on the next level, and up again to rush out through the first available door onto a dimensionless outdoor plaza.

I felt like I had walked through the looking glass into the future. The plaza formed the terminus of a huge, new city being built around the HSR terminal and airport. It had been invisible from inside the terminal but now stretched as far as I could see. A perfect city of neat tree-lined boulevards, bike lanes, well-designed office complexes and street-animating shopping centers. All completely empty, with the surreal feel of *The Truman Show* or one of Jacques Tati's futurist urbanscapes. I walked past the shops looking for somewhere to eat and found just one occupied place, a pastiche of a San Francisco coffee bar clinging to the edge of a Gucci-filled but people-empty complex boldly called The Hub—Connected Greatness. The staff were happy to see me.

I cannot fathom the development economics of this fully finished but barely occupied new city center. Certainly, no other world city or development company could afford it. All through my visit, I was being counselled by Westerners about an impending debt crisis set to engulf China at all levels: government, corporate and personal. There is no shortage of evidence on the ground and Hongqiao would have to be a leading example of massive public and private investment requiring an extremely long horizon for any reasonable return. But outsiders lecturing China on indebtedness is a bit rich. Leaving aside the glaring overbuild of Versace and Prada outlets, most of what I was looking at around Hongqiao was solid, growth-positive infrastructure investment of a kind that the West, despite its own mountains of debt, has neglected. Rail terminals, airports, office buildings and bus stations are useful, productive elements of the urban machine that, though rattling empty now, will doubtless be filled in a decade or less given the city's current rate of growth. What we are seeing in China bears many similarities to the successive railroad booms and busts that characterized the settlement of the United States. And Hongqiao? It will soon be a lovely place, enjoyed by many people, I am sure, once it is finished.

* * *

I had asked my staff to search out the kind of restaurant I like when travelling by myself, and luckily Shanghai has plenty. They directed me to a few sites in the French Concession near my hotel and even spelled out their preferred dishes in Chinese. I arrived at a neighborhood place with several different kitchens congregated around a common dining area, with Formica tables that filled at mealtime with families, groups of young workers and the occasional solitary like myself. Not many *gweilo* solitaries, it has to be said. I showed my office guidebook to one of the cooks, pointing out my preference. Delighted, she grabbed it from my hand and walked round the eating area shouting its suggestions. I was possibly the first Canadian they had ever served and, as such, I was a celebrity.

Over the inevitable duck noodle soup prepared in this Chinese mama's kitchen, I review what I have learned about Shanghai. The first and unavoidable conclusion is that I am a crap consultant. I have had a very unproductive week. So many of the meetings did not turn out the way I had expected, the schedule arranged weeks earlier seemed to simultaneously unravel and get tied in knots. There were serious screw-ups for which I searched, unsuccessfully, for someone else to blame. I had spent much of the time on my own, wandering around the city with a slightly floaty feeling. Shanghai is flat, a frequent misty smog closes off the sun and the view. That and the absence of Google maps reacquainted me with the twisted pleasures of getting lost. I did so every day somewhere, emerging each time from an identical subway stop in a completely different part of the city. I had given up my normal habits since being here: wine, beer, red meat, bread, sugar, dairy, all gone. Their absence filled me with a liberating, manic energy as I walked around day and night, stopping only for bowls of duck noodle soup. I had no digital access, no news. My screens were frozen on the day I arrived. My mobile phone exhausted itself searching for my email account.

The more important conclusion is this: I am convinced that Shanghai is destined for global supremacy. Three connected reasons: its muscular city-building strategy, its colossal scale and the entrepreneurial energy of its citizens. I have talked about the effectiveness of Shanghai's city planning. What is just as significant is its newness. Other great cities are still reliant upon the infrastructure of their periods of peak development, the great Victorian city-building legacy of European cities and the Eisenhower-era interstate highway developments of North America. That essential urban equipment, built by each generation's incarnation of Robert Moses, is getting old, and cities are often unable or unwilling to modernize it. Beyond the physical infrastructure, the city management skills of too many European and North American cities have congealed almost to the point of dysfunction. Shanghai's municipal machine is more productive than its competitors and it clearly demonstrates good government, whether in the form of impeccably clean streets, or the clever public land leases that provide revenue to fund infrastructure projects and social housing. Shanghai has both the economic power and the basic infrastructure to provide a good quality of life for the populations streaming into the city. It is all very top-down, controlled and planned. Prototypical Jane Jacobs stories of small businesses and property owners being chased out by big money and big government abound. But it is hard to see how else the mistakes of every other city in the rapidly urbanizing world could have been avoided. There does, however, seem to be an inexorable logic to city building. It was fascinating to meet the very impressive Xia Liping, head of the Shanghai Planning Institute and responsible for all of the city's long-range planning, who indicated that she felt the process of planning now had to move towards greater public engagement and a more local focus. Towards the production of more home. She's right, of course, but living as I do in a city where no planning thought can be uttered without a public meeting, I wondered whether to warn her. There is no question that it will take longer to build their future subway lines.

It may also be that Shanghai built everything too quickly. There have been post-construction problems with the subway, not surprising perhaps given the subsoil they had to tunnel through. Shanghai is built on millennia of Yangtze Delta alluvium. Everything is sinking and shrinking, a fact that makes the city, at an average elevation of only five meters, highly susceptible to rising sea levels. Shanghai is only five miles from the East China Sea and at high tide, the rusty freighters charging up the Huangpu River between the new raised flood-protection river banks seem to tower over the Bund buildings.

What ultimately determines the success of cities is immigration. In China's case, that migration has been internal, from the countryside to the cities. The government has actively managed the process with its *hukou* residency permit system, but like all such attempts to manage the flow of the rural poor to available urban jobs, it has been only partially effective. About half the population of the city still lacks this long-term residency permit. Indeed, it is on the backs of something resembling the quasi-illegal immigrant class that we met in the Bronx and in Barking that Shanghai's great subway investments and high-rise towers have been built. Of course, it is on their urban energy, their striving, their determination to improve their lives and that of their families that all great cities are built and their futures made. Shanghai simply has more of that energy than anywhere else.

As it grows, Shanghai will have to attract not only China's but the world's best. There is no doubt that it can produce its own creative class. Shanghaiers have an easy familiarity with technology. The city has the highest use of cashless payments of any in the world, and just down the regional rail in Hangzhou is the world headquarters of Alibaba, the huge online retailer that is probably the only rival in the world to Amazon. China, with Shanghai at its center, is positioning itself as the primary producer of high-tech batteries and robots, surely the key manufacturing activities of the rest of the century. Can the city attract others from afar, that floating global intelligentsia and business class seemingly essential for a higher-order city? Probably not yet. Shanghai's leading university, Fudan, ranks 155th in the league tables. The city's cultural offering looks thin and derivative. On the street, Shanghaiers are strivers, not *flaneurs*. But this, too, will change. This old city is still very young. It is steadily emerging as China's premier cultural center, with a lightness of being that Beijing finds hard to muster. Museums and galleries are popping up all over, particularly in the new hip district of the West Bund, several of them funded by the great private wealth the city has created, following the pattern of the Tates, Guggenheims and Fricks in turn-of-the-century English and American cities. Recognizing the economic importance of the creative class, the city has supported it with tax concessions and other inducements under the fine banner of "Culture First, Industry Oriented." We should also remember that in the thirties, Shanghai did have a distinctive international glamour as an anything goes, end-of-empire city. I am not sure this is what the authors of socialist modernization have in mind, but nothing is so permanent as urban character.

The sheer scale of China and its premier cities will exert a force of global economic gravity. In a short time, the country has lifted more people out of poverty than any other nation in the history of the world, employing its particular brand of illiberal capitalism, and its great, exploding cities are a consequence of this magnificent project. The success or failure of the country's next great transformation, from cheap production to sophisticated service and manufacturing economy, will take place in the cities. Will a perhaps inevitable urban democracy grow? There seems some evidence already. Hints of Jane Jacobs sprouting like grass between the paving stones of the overwhelmingly Moses-built city? Big cities always have to broaden their power base, particularly in the contemporary economy. Perhaps Shanghai has another advantage in China unique to great commercial cities: an ability to experiment and take risks, giving it a flexibility unavailable to the other Chinese megalopolises. It is not the capital, Beijing, where an excess of government power seems to have constrained its urbanity. It is not Hong Kong, whose ambiguous governmental status and business culture could limit its influence. And it is not Shenzhen or another of the instant cities that have developed in China in the past three decades. It is a city with a dynamic trading culture and a long sense of itself. It will make its own history. There is a fine Chinese proverb of which Shanghaiers are fond: the mountains are high, and the emperor is far away.

The cook brings me another bowl of duck noodle soup and beams to the crowd. Delightful, but I have been on the road far too long. I am weary to my bones. It is beyond time to go home. Our journey is done.

11

AND THE PERFECT CITY IS. . .?

S o, let us imagine that we are sitting on a bench in a fine park in a striving global city, with Jane Jacobs on one side and Robert Moses on the other. "What makes the perfect city? Which of you is right? What have we learned from our world urban tour?" Moses leans in with that strong, imperious face. Jacobs squawks with derision. And, of course, we would not get a word in, both of them being New Yorkers, locked in an argument that has gone on too long. As our walk around world cities shows, the answers lie in the spaces between. Top down or bottom up? Both. Small-scale organic or large-scale structural intervention? Both. Bike lanes or high-speed intra-city transport. Both. City growth or community cohesion? Both. And surely the most important conclusion: you cannot have one without the other.

Perhaps we should leave them on the bench to continue their ever-instructive squabble as the life of the city flows by. Their questions still linger. What inherited and acquired urban character, what combination of good management and good luck, which accidents and interventions best aspire to perfection? But things have moved on, and so should we. We need to return to the themes established at the outset. Cities are big, complicated places. What have we learned?

What the best-managed cities must do first is care for the urban machine: good city builders need to be good mechanics and confidently operate at the scale of the real functioning city. The best city is one that can most effectively support the creation of the collective employment and wealth necessary to support its residents' lives and aspirations, that can readily move people and goods around, that can connect broadly to the wider world, that can continuously build and rebuild its ever-changing physical structure and best capture global forces of economic change and investment. That is the machine. It is the precondition. Neither home nor delight can be found if it is not working well. Cities can decline, either precipitously like Detroit or industrial Manchester, or slowly like St. Louis and Chicago, or functionally like Toronto and New York. Urban decline is far more problematic than growth. It cannot be fixed with small actions alone. Do not let it happen.

Of course, that machine is also home—home to its residents, to the old and young, to new immigrants and long-time residents. The search for and guardianship of home is one of the most powerful of human emotions. In the big cities of the world, that home seems increasingly hard to find. Flows of immigration are increasing while racial and nationalist tension and violence appear to be on the rise after years of decline in many cities. The seemingly inherent spikiness of current global city economy is exacerbating income inequality. That same spikiness has infected big-city housing markets, most extremely in the most successful cities, opening them to pressures that are destroying affordability for the average citizen, constraining the city's ability to welcome the very people who make it work. If city residents new and old cannot make a home in a city, watch out. There is no greater source of trouble.

So, machine, yes. Home, yes. But there is more. For all of human history, people have gone to cities for their sheer delight. For freedom, for sex, for the jolt to the spine at first seeing the Eiffel Tower, first walking down Broadway or crossing Westminster Bridge at midnight and looking back. For all the smaller pleasures, the smell, noise, taste, sounds; the light and dark, solid and void, street and building, the hard and soft of a city. Urban delight is part accident, part fabrication. There are no rules. It is largely, although not entirely, a matter of individual taste. As in all great art, the skill of making a good city is to conceal the artifice.

Let us start with the machine, with the need for cities to take big bold actions to ensure economic success, make deep investments in infrastructure, and constantly regenerate its physical fabric. What have we learned? That too many European and North American cities, partly as a result of Jane Jacobs-ism, but as much because of wider political, economic, demographic and cultural forces, have lost the nerve and capacity to undertake the projects that are necessary for their futures, and that cities in Asia are showing the way. A simplification, but largely true. City planning in too many European and North American cities seems to be trapped in small concerns, unable or unwilling to grasp the big levers.

The transit systems and airports of Singapore, Shanghai and Hong Kong lead the world in the boldness of their scale, technology and management. They undoubtedly had two great advantages: relatively cheap labor and the absence of a pre-existing, outmoded system, enabling a quick leap to the leading edge. But as important was the firm governmental hand that directed these projects to be accomplished. In varying degrees, these three cities are city-states. They have the urban command and control necessary to undertake big projects. The mature European and North American cities, as we saw in New York, Manchester and, to some extent, Toronto, once had that confidence and are struggling to regain it.

New York's transit system suffers from a crippling split jurisdiction between city and state, best exemplified by the sixty years it took to build a short section of the Second Avenue subway. The key commuter hub of Penn Station is at a point of imminent meltdown, with regular closures from derailments and signal failures, reflecting decades of under-maintenance and lack of investment. My own Toronto region has been unable to invest in or manage its transit at anything like the scale the growing city requires, held back by the lack of an overall unitary authority capable of making and implementing the necessary long-term decisions and raising the required financing.

Of the cities we visited outside Asia, only London continues to inspire confidence in its ability to undertake large-scale innovative transit projects, showing the way with its continuing ability to not only plan and build city-changing, new, high-speed intra-city subway lines like Crossrail 1 and 2, but at the same time investing in and innovating with its existing transit system. It was the first big city to implement a congestion charge, the first European city to create an interactive transit pass (and then supplement it with credit card and phone tap access), to re-invent its bus service, to provide real-time information at every bus stop, to introduce driverless trains, to think about the transit rider as a valued customer rather than as everyday human baggage. Transport for London, TfL as it is known, is perfect. One prize, however, still waits to be awarded. A wave of disruption is hitting urban movement systems. For the first time in decades, public transit ridership is beginning to drop. The city that can comprehensively re-invent its urban movement systems to a zero-carbon, driverless vehicle, smart-city, public/private financed and operated, user-pay, drone-friendly future—that will be the exemplar of this century. In all probability, that will be a new world city.

With respect to airports, much the same story can be told. Former U.S. Vice-President Joe Biden once famously described New York's La Guardia as a "third world airport," though the comparison is largely inaccurate, as we have seen from the stellar initiatives in that once third world. La Guardia, Newark and JFK are home-grown American examples of the steady and widespread decay of U.S. urban infrastructure. To be fair, the Port Authority of New York and New Jersey, which controls all the region's airports, is undertaking a massive and impressive refit of La Guardia—but it still will not have direct connection to the subway system. Meanwhile, Heathrow's addition of a third runway seems forever constrained by well-organized opposition. Sydney's current international airport looks tired but New South Wales has finally determined to start work on a new one to the west of its urban region. If it can proceed successfully, it will be one of the few Western cities to have developed a new airport, others unable to overcome local resident opposition despite the critical importance of airports to the contemporary city economy.

The exception in the first world group would probably have to be Toronto Pearson, growing even faster than the city it serves and expanding in both volume and connectivity to join the top half-dozen international hubs. It is a publicly owned facility but cleverly managed at arm's length from both local and national political concerns, and it is about to undertake that hardest of tasks—following the impressive formula that Manchester Airport put together and drawing in massive private investment for a substantial expansion while still serving its public purpose. It is *en route* to perfection.

Along with the key infrastructure of transit and airports, our international city tour demonstrated the central role of universities as developers of human capital and catalysts for stimulating, directly and indirectly, the innovation and entrepreneurial economies. All the cities we visited have established universities now fixated on stepping up in the global rankings. Why? Cities are run on brains—remember the advice of Singapore's city leader—not on natural resources, not even on business or manufacturing, but on the competitive smarts of its citizens. While not all entrepreneurs or city builders come out of the best universities, an extraordinary number of those responsible for the developing economy of a city does. The key mechanism of the modern city will be joining those brains to the process of wealth creation.

Many cities have undertaken impressive programs to stimulate their innovation economy, although each following their unique path, as illustrated by the completely different strategies of New York, Singapore, London and Toronto. New York's development of Cornell Tech has set the standard for the shortest time period between conception and realization of an impressive piece of intellectual infrastructure. In just seven years, the city executed the procurement, design, financing and construction of a project intended to fill an identified gap in the city's economic machine. It was breathtakingly perfect, and it delivered a wake-up kick to New York's other universities.

Singapore's strategy is more corporate, as represented by the scope of the comprehensive innovation complex at One North, with its stylish new buildings and landscaping. London's is more diffuse and aimed at individual businesses, with programs to support an eastward vector of renovated industrial buildings full of old and new companies, running from Kings Cross to Queen Elizabeth Park. Toronto innovated with its impressive MaRS project and has sensibly focused on ensuring the best-trained STEM workforce in the world. Its excellent, accessible public education system at all levels may indeed be the smartest investment a city can make. Tech companies seem increasingly driven in their locational decisions by the availability of the necessary trained workforce, rather than by office rental costs or other factors. Had Sydney been able to pull off its remake of the White Bay Power Station as the core of an innovation cluster fueling a total makeover of their empty port lands, it would have become the poster child for the next decade. That honor is now waiting to be seized. As their experience demonstrated, cities now have to learn how to deal with the increasing oligopolistic power of the big tech companies—essentially the economic equivalents of the auto plants of the past century—requiring a very sophisticated understanding of urban management.

It is easy to grind one's teeth at the ethical shortcomings of the tech and financial sectors, but that's an unaffordable indulgence for any city once it realizes how important those sectors are to its economic machine. They typically comprise the largest and highest-value sector of urban economies, and carry the greatest multiplier effects for other businesses, whether direct or indirect. The financial sector in particular typically pays a significant share of national and local property, corporate and personal income taxes. Banks and financial institutions also establish their presences in a city in innumerable indirect ways. Just look at all those corporate logos on the cultural or community events you attend, or the make-up of boards of large cultural, medical and social service institutions. Part of the difficulty lower-tier cities have in advancing their arts scenes or fundraising for their local hospital is the lack of deep pockets that the tech and financial services sectors bring.

The best example of managing these key sectors of the urban economy has to be the development of Canary Wharf and the arc of financial services and tech activity that now connects the east of London back to the west, providing what was once an inaccessible part of the city with five different transit connections. Canary Wharf is also a poster child for the key concept of inclusive growth, deliberately fostering connections to the local community and workforce, now accounting for 54 per cent of the jobs in the local borough, once one of the poorest in London, and at the same time doubling its workforce. The tech sector has made similar connections to local educational institutions.

The key question is whether the inherent spikiness of these sectors will endure. In some form or another, they are always vulnerable to disruptive challenges. Fin-tech innovation, for instance, could radically change the type of buildings in which the financial services industry works, and the required numbers and skills of its labor force. Those trends are already underway—only half of Canary Wharf's workforce is now involved in traditional financial services, the rest in various forms of fin-tech or media activities. But the contemporary global city workforce seems to be changing its skills rather than shrinking; there is no evidence that Richard Florida's winner-take-all economy is diminishing. These connections between the cause and effects of city building create much of the difficulty in city management. It is clear, however, that you cannot have the job creation, the transit construction, the community benefits and the public infrastructure unless you accommodate an urban economy on a scale that makes those consequences possible. It does not work the other way around. Moses precedes Jacobs.

The recent city competition to be awarded the location housing the 50,000 jobs slated for the second Amazon headquarters complex brings all these issues into sharp focus. The up-side of winning is clear: that number of good jobs will be transformative even in the largest of cities. The downside for any winning city, especially for the smaller cities on the list, is the powerful impact that all those new, well-paid workers will have on housing prices and cost of living—we saw the average income of London's Google workers of about $300,000; the average for the much larger number of Amazon workers is slated at $100,000. Which raises the question of whether the constraint of ever-ascending property prices will eventually blunt the spikes? Unlikely, but there could be an impact on the form of the megacity that houses them. Businesses that require intensive amounts of human capital locate where they can attract the right labor pool. That used to be in the suburbs; now it is clearly in the central city. If the mostly young incoming workforce cannot afford to live there, those new jobs may have to follow employees out to the places they can afford. London is beginning to shed jobs to its satellite cities of Reading, Bristol, Bath and Cardiff. Much the same can be seen around New York, where the once-moribund cities of Newark, White Plains, Norwalk and Bridgepoint are adding significant employment. For the first time in living memory, more workers are commuting out of rather than into Manhattan, and into rather than out of those satellite cities. This pattern of a dispersed, multi-centered metropolis well connected to a core global hub seems to be the emerging structure of the new urban economy. Its success depends on good transit, re-emphasizing the need for capable regional management. The solution to the megacity housing crisis lies to a significant extent at the end of high-speed, intra-urban rail, bringing lower-priced housing within the metropolitan market.

This is good news and bad news for smaller and intermediate-size cities. If you are within an hour of the metropolis, its airports and universities, you are likely to be the beneficiary of this new urban structure. If you are more than a couple of hours away, your prospects for growth are not good. Overall there is no reason to believe that the spikiness of metropolitan economies is going to diminish. If anything, the converse is true. Richard Florida recently found that the world's fifty largest cities, home to only 7 per cent of the world's population, generate 40 per cent of its economic growth.

It will be fascinating to watch the churn that will occur between the short list of top financial and innovation centers over the next decades. The global pattern of spikiness may also be in flux. Europe's long-term structural decline in global economic importance and the probable erosion of London's role post-Brexit would suggest that only one European financial center of significance may be required, and that of secondary importance to the rest of the world. The long-term consequences of President Trump's anti-immigrant and anti-free trade initiatives may not be enough to destabilize New York but they will contribute to Chicago's anemic population growth as its older economy drops in the rankings.

Hong Kong is becoming increasingly uncertain for international business. To slip from the spike has serious consequences for a city, given the economic energy generated by the financial and tech sectors. The rising, increasingly organized economies of China and India will both want a national urban focus for their economic power, most likely in Shanghai and Mumbai respectively. Shanghai is the place most obviously ready and has already moved rapidly into the top ten financial centers group. When the consequent multiplier effect of becoming such a concentrated financial hub takes hold and combines with that city's remarkable lead in tech and advanced manufacturing, Shanghai will rise to an increasingly central world role, perhaps even to become the leading city. It could not happen to a more capable place.

The optimal functioning of the urban machine is the precondition for the successful city. Its imperatives are ignored at peril. How, therefore, to resolve the reality that the machine has to provide home for those who work in it? Sadly, that is something fewer and fewer cities are managing to do well. Two large-scale sorting processes seem to be at work. The first we have seen within the megacities, of the rising disparities of income and wealth and the seeming increasing separation of those urban areas between the rich and the rest. A perhaps more unsettling trend is the growing separation between those cities, with all their internal disparities and conflicts, and the hinterland out of reach of the megacity economy. The geographic distribution of the Brexit vote brought that metropolitan/non-metropolitan split into sharp relief. Anti-European sentiment was strongest in those deprived parts of the U.K. that were, in fact, the greatest recipients of EU financial assistance by virtue of that deprivation; anti-immigrant sentiment strongest in places with the fewest immigrants. That's what happens when the urban machine fails, a pattern repeated in the 2016 U.S. presidential election.

Is it nonetheless possible to find encouragement, given the dynamic strength of metropolitan life? In most Western countries, despite these recent electoral setbacks, the young, urban, multi-ethnic, educated, cosmopolitan, "open" sector of the population is already at or close to a majority and is growing in size. The older, white, non-urban, poorly-educated, localist, "closed" sector is in decline. Another cause for hope is the organized way in which major U.S. cities are maintaining, in contemporary versions, their dreams of "the city on the hill" with the kind of sanctuary city programs we saw in the Bronx.

That is not to say that a lot of damage will not be done in what one hopes is the last blast of the pre-metropolitan trumpet. Policies to restrict new immigration and deport undocumented immigrants, the substantial majority of whom are long-term productive residents of the United States, are not only inhumane, they will deal a body blow to the high tech, medical and professional sectors, as well as to the agricultural, hospitality and tourism mainstays of the economy. Indeed, if my New York restaurateur friend's experience is anything to go by, one would believe that much of the Trump hotel and casino workforce would have to be sent home. In New York City, it has been estimated that more than 10 per cent of the population is undocumented. These people do work no one else will do. They pay taxes. They just get none of the benefits. An equally destructive urban policy is the administration's restriction on special visas to admit highly qualified immigrants. Those striving global brains will go somewhere else.

The resistance to immigration is not only an issue for European, North American and Australian cities. As we saw, the exploding centers of Asia exhibit similar strains. In the almost one-party, near-perfect state of Singapore, the strongest political stress seems not in the direction of greater political freedom or cultural liberalization but in anti-immigrant feeling. Non-status residents amount to a fifth of the residents. They are the house cleaners and construction laborers, temporary workers brought in from Indonesia and the Philippines. In Shanghai, one-third of residents do not have a *hukou* permit for long-term citizenship. The strength of the Asian economies has so far enabled those cities to avoid the tensions prevalent in Europe and the US. How long can that last?

Why is the successful management of immigration a key factor in urban success, why is it the most important indicator of urban perfection? Because a big city's core activity is and has always been, to help those self-selected few who have fled their countries or the countryside to transform themselves into contented, productive citizens in their new homes. The basic economic rules—buy cheap, add value, sell dear—are as true for people as for things.

Great cities need to recognize their self-interest in continued immigration and to make new citizens welcome. If there is one lesson that Belfast leaves us it is that, although the smallest, least economically significant city we visited, it has made the most impressive shift of urban culture, from closed- to open-hearted. It stopped fighting. All cities can learn from that.

Toronto is the closest to perfection in making urban immigrants feel at home. Again, the numbers are remarkable. The Toronto region accepts between 100,000 and 125,000 new immigrants a year, making it by far the most welcoming of any city in the developed world, not only relative to its size but absolutely. Most newcomers arrive through the national immigration process with its structured system of acceptance through qualifications, language ability and family contacts. Another mass of newcomers arrives as refugees, driven to Canada by convulsions in their homelands. Interestingly, the future success of new citizens in the country does not seem to vary greatly between the two sources, which speaks to the qualities of the people themselves, to their self-direction and motive power to get up and go. Which is why urban immigration is usually successful, provided that the receiving city is prepared to make the newcomers feel at home. The library card received on entry to the country, all those required language classes, the English as a second language skills taught by the school systems, together with the quality and accessibility of schools, a universally accessible public health system, child benefit payments, good minimum pensions, good, inexpensive public universities—the successful city has to have this human equipment, this basic social infrastructure, and share it with its new citizens. It recognizes and supports the reality that not only are strong families the single most important social component of a city, but they are also its critical economic unit. Economically liberal, community-supportive social democracy is coming under increasing criticism from both left and right, but it works. It is the best, most productive way to organize an urban society.

A recent example makes the point perfectly. Waterfront Toronto, the agency responsible for developing the city's lakefront, is currently engaged in an interesting experiment with Sidewalk Labs, an offshoot of Alphabet, Google's parent company, to re-invent the contemporary city on a parcel of harbor land. Sidewalk is headed by the energizing Dan Doctoroff, my former deputy-mayor client in New York. What will actually emerge from this exercise is anyone's guess. The city's various thought communities are adopting their characteristic stance of cautious negativity, but the experiment is nonetheless exciting, potentially offering an integrated urban expertise that itself could become an export industry. At the project's gala kick-off, Prime Minister Trudeau was followed to the podium by Eric Schmidt, Google's founder, as nerdy a guy as you could meet, despite being the 119th wealthiest man in the world. Why did he pick Toronto for this exercise, he was asked? "We looked at over fifty cities worldwide. We picked Toronto for a lot of reasons. But if there is one thing I know from running Google, it is that innovation is fueled by immigration." If Toronto can embrace the Sidewalk opportunity without having its pockets picked in the Amazon fashion, that will be a singular urban achievement.

Unique cultures of inclusion and entrepreneurship are emerging from a comparable acceptance of immigrant culture in London, New York and Manchester, with their conscious fostering of diverse music festivals, multicultural celebrations and the internationalist faces they present to the world. Toronto, however, does it best, and nowhere does it seem to happen so unselfconsciously. Perhaps, again, this is due to sheer numbers. Toronto is well beyond the tipping point at which the presence of new immigrants becomes a substantial facet of urban life—that seems to happen when a city is around one-third newcomers. When it gets to Toronto's level, where a majority were not born in the country and more than half are visible minority, something entirely new is taking place. A community not based on ethnicity but on a new shared idea of what constitutes citizenship.

These days, the biggest threat to the creation of a durable and satisfying home in the global city is the cost of housing. To do something significant about the problem requires boldness. There is no doubt that Singapore's unique, almost universal public housing/private ownership strategy has delivered affordable mass housing to its population in the face of intense housing pressures, but it is probably not a readily transferable system. In more liberal market cultures New York probably has the edge on London, although both are impressive. Both have aggressively opened former port and industrial lands and mandated realistic mixes of residential and commercial development. Both have used the planning system to incentivize the kind of housing they want and discourage what they do not want. Both have stimulated rental rather than condo development and both have looked after their existing affordable stock reasonably well. The numbers bear this out: both cities have almost doubled their overall as well as their affordable housing production in the past decade, although New York has been more adventurous in their techniques of social housing financing. They can share a working-on-perfection prize, with the edge to New York. On a smaller scale, Manchester has cleverly leveraged its city land holdings to attract long-term foreign investors in new rental housing. Neither Toronto or Sydney have done much at the necessary scale to increase their affordable housing supply or to manage their housing markets. They are both storing up big trouble.

Which brings us to the big question about large-scale city initiatives. Why can some cities execute them and others not? Our tour suggests two reasons: governance and geography. City governments, more so than other levels of government, actually do things. They run the buses and the trains, build the sewers, pick up the garbage and manage the housing estates. National governments may set overarching financial, taxation and legislative policy, and deliver a lot of pension checks, but their day-to-day interactions with the citizenry are limited. Even state or provincial governments in federal systems tend to rely on cities to implement their housing, educational and social assistance programs. As a result, cities, unlike senior levels of government, typically develop localist, service-driven political cultures, something reinforced by their typically ward-based political systems.

There is a downside to this community responsiveness. It frustrates the longer-term, large-scale strategizing and delivery that urban economies require. It is inadequate for managing the urban machine and unresponsive to on-going commitments to maintain and expand the urban home. As importantly, it lacks the scale and competence for effective action against climate change, income inequality, urban terrorism and spiraling costs of living. These are all now metropolitan concerns as much as—if not more than—national issues, requiring metropolitan responsiveness. This crisis of urban management becomes particularly acute as cities merge into megalopolises; it almost seems as if a city of a few million can muddle along. An urban area approaching or exceeding ten million absolutely has to manage itself.

The optimal form of urban governance is therefore one that can combine the strength and consistency of purpose required for undertaking large projects with the local contact necessary for civic harmony. The practical evidence suggests this requires a two-tiered structure: local councils that can respond directly to residents' concerns, and a central executive body led by an empowered mayor, supported by capable deputy mayors, with the authority and political insulation to take big, expensive, long-term decisions. Robert Moses works for the upper tier. Jane Jacobs advises the boroughs.

London's governance structure consists of a Greater London Authority comprised of elected politicians from the thirty-three local boroughs, along with some mayoral appointees, and a mayor elected at large by all Londoners. New York has a directly elected mayor with extensive powers, supported by selected deputy mayors, and a city council consisting of the mayors of the city's five boroughs. Although the precise menu of powers and responsibilities between the four big urban actors—the mayor, the deputy mayors, the assembly/city council and the borough councils—varies somewhat between London and New York, the essential principles apply. Big things are managed by the top tier and local stuff by the boroughs. This division of powers fits with the natural proclivities of politicians at both levels, and it also reflects the way cities work, accommodating the inherent tensions between big and small urban affairs. Even in that very top-down, governmental-controlled city of Shanghai, a two-tier governance system is emerging for just those reasons. The year 2017 marked the relaunch, after three decades, of a Greater Manchester Assembly, with a directly elected mayor and a council made up of the eleven mayors of surrounding cities, boroughs and towns, to give it the heft required to become the second metropolis of the U.K.

We have seen several examples of how important strong leadership is in the perfect city. If only Bloomberg, De Blasio, Sadiq Khan and Lee Kuan Yew ruled the urban world. A mayor with the power to do things and the ability to assemble a team of capable doers is the prerequisite for urban success. The increasing importance of city government is evident the world over, reflective of the steady urbanization of the economy, along with the gradual retreat of national governments, perhaps for political or ideological reasons, or perhaps because in today's culture and economy, they can no longer attract the talent. The big test for the next generation of cities will however be whether they have the maturity and political strength to levy the taxes necessary to support their increased responsibilities. There are encouraging signs from unlikely places, including Los Angeles and Salt Lake City, where citizens have voted to tax themselves to fund new public transit. There are equivalently discouraging signs from Toronto.

The other advantage of the big/small urban political structure is that it allows for the management of the full geography of the real city. The City of New York is responsible for about three-quarters of its urban region, the Greater London Council for slightly more. The newly reconstituted governance of the Paris region has created the Métropole de Grand Paris, another two-tier structure coordinating 131 communes, which has a geography extending to the limits of that metropolitan area. No urban boundary is ever entirely satisfactory. You can make a case that all of central England is an economic extension of London, in the same way that Boston might be an economic suburb of New York City. More realistically, from a functional point of view, the optimal city government should encompass the substantial majority of its commuter-shed. It is the journey to work that sets the pattern of housing, employment and the transit network necessary to connect them. It also defines the economic region that can be effectively managed,

spurred and marketed, as well as the most coherent cultural community and, not unimportantly, the geography of loyalty to sports teams.

The governance structures of the cities of Toronto and Sydney bear
no relation to their urban geography or to their pressing agendas. The
lack of an over-arching government has visible consequences. Both
cities have underdeveloped transit systems, high levels of traffic congestion and uncontrollable housing markets. Neither city effectively
markets itself as a globally competitive city, reflecting the absence of
a properly empowered, regionally effective government. Nobody is
responsible for the whole city. Toronto's remarkable, if accidental, rise
to a global position could founder on this political rock. It cannot find
success as the soon-to-be second largest city of the U.S. and Canada
without proper governance. Sydney, by virtue of being effectively the
ward of New South Wales, may muddle through.

This stress on urban governance is critical but it cannot be allowed
to overshadow another conclusion of our city tour. The importance of
individuals. There is something in the chemistry of a great city that
gives rise to the amazing people who direct its future, arriving often
in the nick of time. It is a seeming contradiction in all the complexity of city building, but unless one person wakes up in the middle of
the night and knows that only they are responsible for making something happen, it won't happen. "Cometh the hour, cometh the man,"
goes the adage, except that in the contemporary city it is more often
the woman. As we saw in city after city—Singapore, London, Belfast,
Manchester, New York and Toronto—it is women who are increasingly in charge. The perfect twenty-first-century city will be their
creation.

And, finally, there is delight—urban delight. We searched in our
cities, never sure of where to find it. In a specific building, a special
place, a neighborhood, a district, a park, along the waterfront, on the
river? Is it in the smell of a fresh-washed sidewalk in the early morning,
or of fresh-baked bagels in the bakery, or that utterly distinctive odor
of electricity in each of the London, Paris and New York subways? In
my city, is it the sound of snow plows in the middle of the night, the
screech of a streetcar making its turn, the collective giggles of children

in the schoolyard beside our office? Is it at a citizenship ceremony in the inner suburbs?

I am suspicious of the contemporary search for grand urban beauty. Many crimes have been committed in its name. In the modern era, such beauty seems to require those signature cultural and civic buildings that arrive like spaceships in city after city. Frank Gehry's Guggenheim Museum in Bilbao, one of the last century's great works of art, became a destination that single-handedly raised the GDP of the Basque region of Spain by a couple of percentage points. It was the Sydney Opera House of its time. But it also has a lot to answer for. It has spawned terrible imitations. The U.K. had a rash of millennium-funded galleries, museums and performance halls, each with its own version of look-at-me architecture. The majority are now closed or struggling. Few had the desired regenerative effect. Toronto produced six new cultural buildings around the same time. Did they have the desired urban stimulus? Maybe, although in retrospect the focus on the traditional arts of opera, ballet and classical music may not have been wise. And several of the buildings, including the inexcusably self-indulgent Royal Ontario Museum extension designed by Daniel Libeskind, the one-trick Ontario College of Art and Design by Will Alsop, and the budget-pinched, neighbor-dampened Art Gallery of Ontario by local boy Frank Gehry, look tired after barely a decade. Interestingly, the buildings designed more modestly by the city's own architects, including Jack Diamond's Opera House, Bruce Kuwabara's Ballet School and Marianne McKenna's Koerner Hall, seem to have matured more gracefully, settling well into their respective neighborhoods.

Who has best managed big city delight in the cities we have seen? Probably Manchester. It started with Bridgewater Hall, a concert hall well situated between the canal and the city center, then added a dramatic signature performance hall and gallery, the Lowry Centre, right out on a prow of the Salford docklands where it acted as a beacon for mixed-use development. Back in the city center, Manchester renovated a former railway station and its associated warehouse buildings into the U.K.'s premier conference and convention center, and it is just about to proceed with a dramatic contemporary cultural center, The

Factory, appropriately on the site of Granada TV's famed *Coronation Street* set. Why the best? Because each of the cultural interventions works in its context, each had a clear economic objective, because the "wow" was limited to where the "wow" would best work and because there is something distinctly Manchester about all of the new buildings, despite the range of architects and locations. Some use the local red brick, others highlight a renowned local artist, or celebrate the city's famed music scene, or mash up new architecture with glorious old structures. Each new building has the sense of being one in a series in which the city reveals itself to the future. Perfect.

Given the problems of grand urban beauty, cities would do well to stimulate delight on a smaller scale, that of the street, the park, the neighborhood. They need to continue to rebalance their streets towards pedestrians and cyclists. They need active street-related retail and new developments of an approachable scale. They need more parks, big and small, to soften the scale of such rapid urbanization. In the cities we have visited, Shanghai's riverfront parks and promenades, part flood protection, part concealed parking, and an interesting unfolding of special retail, eating and artistic places, come closest to perfection on this score. A close second would be the remaking of the Hudson River edge from the Battery to 125th Street in New York. The walkway, bikeway, small and large parks constitute a continuous zipper between Manhattan and the river, with that essential urban magic of being simultaneously deserted and packed.

That said, I must confess at the end of the trip to a fatigue with the dominant expressions of small-scale beauty in contemporary cities. Perhaps I have just been travelling too much but the streets and parks of every city I visited are beginning to resemble each other to an unsettling degree, with their cafés, their streetscaping, their bike lanes, their well-designed lamp fixtures and meaningful public art. Even the store mix is similar in the happening parts of every town. Do not misunderstand me, I know where I want to live, and it is well within the goat cheese line. I have done my share of gentrification. But as an expression of place, the centers and desirable neighborhoods of too many of the cities visited are converging into a common metropolitanism, a universal city culture for all big city dwellers. Unwelcome and unwelcoming, "scrubbed clean by wealth." My partner's phrase haunts me. No wonder Brexit and Trump got out the vote.

My fatigue with these scenes is why our search for perfect urban beauty has tried to take us away from the skin deep, out into the ugly, out beyond those parts of the city that still rely for their good looks on a heritage architectural endowment or well-heeled shoppers, out to the suburbs of Singapore, Shanghai, London, New York and Toronto. I have tried to advance the importance, and resilience, of *jolie laide*, ugly beauty. I hear the reader's doubting sigh. I am not sure I have persuaded you.

So be it. It is time for one last meal, and for some music, and, if we are lucky, a drink. We are going back to the library.

This library is just to the east of the Finch/Weston neighborhood we visited in Toronto, on the far side of a busy freeway. It is a lug of a building, set off from the street, surrounded by a big parking lot that is packed. It is Friday night, the last Friday of the month. Freedom Friday. Opening the door, I know this is not what I expect of a library. A lot of loud music and strong cooking smells. One of the librarians is there to greet me. Behind her on the wall is a poster: "If you have just arrived in Canada in the past few weeks, here are the fourteen things you should do." What follows is an utterly sensible action list. Get a Social Insurance number, a Health Card, a Driver's License. Register your kids at the local school, make sure their immunizations are up to date, sign up for a language class. On it goes, a "To Do" list for a new country. The librarian saw me looking. "Think we forgot some?" she smiles. "Have a good meal. Listen to some good music. Have fun." She sees my confusion. "And lighten up!" With that, I am motioned downstairs.

Every last Friday of the month, the library throws open its doors to anyone who wants to share a good meal and music. Nobody knows whose idea this was but now everyone claims it. The idea of filling a library with food and loud music is wonderfully counter-intuitive after decades of scolding signs reading "No Food or Drink Permitted" and "Shhh." It really needs no author.

The lower floor of the library gives out onto a patio. There are barbecues and buffet warming trays. Mostly Caribbean dishes but a couple of Vietnamese and other interesting stuff I have yet to identify. And samosas—Afghan, Punjabi, Sri Lankan, Uzbek. Is there no end to samosas? A good steel drum band of what seem to be remarkably young kids. I kick back on a bench. Could do with a cold beer but probably that is pushing the mandate of the library too far. And the company is good. On a bench at the back of the deck, a tall, gaunt, energetic man is talking vigorously with a striking, big-boned, strong-faced woman. They have been there a while, leaning in, waving fingers. They must know each other well. Maybe too well. Their conversation continues. The sun is going down, presenting a huge color field in the western sky. The patio gives down to a tree-filled gully. Behind the trees lies a tributary of the Humber, Toronto's foundational river, quietly pulling us all together. Perfect.

ACKNOWLEDGEMENTS

There are so many people to thank in the writing of a book spread over so many cities and so many years. It's also important to clarify at the outset that when one writes in the first person about places and projects it can all too easily sound as if I single-handedly made all things urban come to pass. Nothing could be further from the truth. Everything in a city is made by a team, and on many of those teams I have been very much a minor player, often little more than an observer. So the first acknowledgement must be to all the energetic, dedicated, talented city builders with whom I have been privileged to work in all of their fine cities. Many are mentioned in the text; the others, you know who you are.

Special thanks are, however, due to some special people. First to my partners and colleagues at Urban Strategies, who gave me the space and encouragement to write this book. Above all to Frank Lewinberg with whom I started the firm over three decades ago, neither of us ever imagining it would grow into the global urban planning and design practice it has become. Frank has been a constant source of wisdom and friendship. Mary Castel has provided shrewd advice and counsel as the book emerged.

On the cities referenced, I have learned from and been helped by many. Deserving of special mention are Mark Kleinman, Eddie Smith, Mike Emmerich, Michael Dennis, Dorothy McIntosh, Michael Mendelson, David Wolfe, Tom McKnight, See Nin Tan, Mary Rowe,

Jennifer Sun, Yiwen Zhu and my China explainer, Cecelia Zhong. Leah Birnbaum took on the role of fact checker, but her careful, challenging thinking provided much more. Any remaining errors of fact or opinion are still firmly mine. In long walks, talks and sails, three good friends—John Farrow, Peter Spry-Leverton and, above all, Alan Broadbent—provided vigorous sounding boards as the book took shape.

Beverley Slopen, my agent, has been trying to get me to write a book for too many years and deserves great thanks for her persistence. Ken Whyte, my publisher, must be thanked for taking a chance on the book at the launch of his exciting new publishing venture, The Sutherland House.

My wife Billie died as I was finishing *Perfect City*. My true critic, encouragement, love and friend, she gave me Paris, London and New York, without which this book would never have been born.

ABOUT THE AUTHOR

J oe Berridge, a partner at Urban Strategies, has played a key role in some of the largest and most complex urban regeneration campaigns in the world. He is an accomplished master-planner of city centers, airports, waterfronts, and university campuses, with landmark projects in capitals throughout North America and Europe. A frequent contributor to The Globe and Mail and the Literary Review of Canada, he is an Adjunct Professor in the Program in Planning at the University of Toronto and a Fellow in the Munk School of Public Policy. *Perfect City* is his first book

INDEX